Philip Schaff

The Epistle of Paul to the Galatians

Philip Schaff

The Epistle of Paul to the Galatians

ISBN/EAN: 9783337729370

Printed in Europe, USA, Canada, Australia, Japan

Cover: Foto ©Lupo / pixelio.de

More available books at **www.hansebooks.com**

THE EPISTLE OF PAUL

TO THE

GALATIANS.

NEW YORK, *February, 1881.*

DEAR SIR:

I beg you to accept a complimentary copy of my Commentary on the Galatians, in advance of its publication.

Believe me, very truly yours,

PHILIP SCHAFF.

THE

EPISTLE OF PAUL

TO THE

GALATIANS.

EXPLAINED BY

PHILIP SCHAFF, D. D.,

BALDWIN PROFESSOR OF SACRED LITERATURE IN THE UNION THEOLOGICAL SEMINARY AT NEW YORK.

[TO BE PUBLISHED IN VOL. III. OF "SCHAFF'S ILLUSTRATED
POPULAR COMMENTARY."]

NEW YORK:
CHARLES SCRIBNER'S SONS.
1881.

The Riverside Press, Cambridge:
Printed by H. O. Houghton and Company.

TABLE OF CONTENTS.

PREFACE.

THE Epistle to the Galatians is an inspired vindication of the independent authority and the free gospel of the Apostle of the Gentiles against his Judaizing opponents. It gives the deepest inside view into the fermentation and commotion of the primitive church. It reveals, in clearer and stronger colors than any other book of the New Testament, both the difference and the harmony among the Apostles; a difference ignored by the old orthodoxy which saw only the harmony, and exaggerated by modern skepticism which denies the harmony. It anticipates, in grand fundamental outlines, a conflict which is renewed from time to time in the history of the church. It is the great charter of Christian liberty, and the Gibraltar of evangelical Protestantism. Under this banner the Reformers fought and triumphed against the legal and ceremonial bondage of the papacy which reproduced, on a larger scale and in the name of St. Peter, the errors and intrigues of the Judaizing party of the Apostolic age. At the same time the Epistle contains the key-note of a final Irenicon of all doctrinal and ritualistic controversies, in the sentence: "In Christ Jesus neither circumcision availeth anything, nor uncircumcision, but faith working through love" (v. 6); "Neither is circumcision anything, nor uncircumcision, but a new creature. And as many as shall walk by this rule, peace be upon them, and mercy, and upon the Israel of God" (vi. 16).

It is my duty and privilege to explain this and other books of the Bible to my students. Twenty years ago I published two chapters of this Commentary, as a specimen of the "Popular Commentary on the New Testament," of which it now forms a part. The plan, the translation, and the comments are substantially the same, but revised and improved, with the aid of ancient and modern commentators, and with reference to the historical and critical controversies which cluster around the second chapter of this Epistle as related to the fifteenth chapter of the Acts. I am especially indebted to Meyer (5th and 6th editions), Wieseler, Ellicott, and Lightfoot. Nor would I forget the stimulating and suggestive value of the critical labors of Baur, Hilgenfeld, and Holsten, although I widely differ from them.

The popular aim forbids lengthy comments, but the more difficult problems of the Epistle are discussed in brief essays which will make the English reader acquainted with some of the most important topics of controversy in the history of the Apostolic age.

PHILIP SCHAFF.

NEW YORK (Union Theological Seminary), *January, 1881.*

THE

EPISTLE TO THE GALATIANS.

INTRODUCTION.

§ 1. THE GALATIANS. § 2. THE CONVERSION OF THE GALATIANS. § 3. OCCASION OF THE EPISTLE. § 4. OBJECT AND CONTENTS. § 5. TIME AND PLACE OF COMPOSITION. § 6. CHARACTER AND VALUE OF THE EPISTLE. § 7. GENUINENESS.

§ 1. *The Galatians.*

GALATIA or GALLO-GRÆCIA was a mountainous but fertile province in the interior of Asia Minor. It had its name from the Gallic or Celtic tribes which inhabited it.[1] Their ancestors, on invitation of Nicomedes, king of Bithynia, had come from the left banks of the Rhine and the Moselle, and, in company with a small number of Germans, settled in Asia about 280 before Christ.[2] This was a backward movement in the migration of nations, which usually follows the westward course of the sun, but is occasionally repulsed or voluntarily recedes. In Galatia these emigrants from Gaul mingled with Greeks,[3] and acquired their language, but retained the partial use of their vernacular tongue, which resembled the Germanic (or Celtic) dialect of the region of Treves on the Moselle, as spoken in the fourth century.[4] They were the terror and scourge of Asia Minor, but after

---

[1] *Galatians, Gauls, Celts,* are often used synonymously by ancient writers. The Scotch Highlanders still call their own country *Gulatia* (*Gaëldachd*), the land of the Gauls (Gaels). So says Dr. MacGregor, who is a native of the Scotch Highlands, *Com. on Galat.* (Edinb. 1879), p. 14. Jerome derives the name of the Galatians from the whiteness of their complexion (γάλα), described by Virgil.

[2] The *Germani cisrhenani,* on the left side of the Rhine, were sometimes included among the Gauls. The names of the leaders of the Asiatic expedition, *Lutarius* (the Saxon *Luther,* the French *Lothaire*) and *Leonnorius,* seem to be German ; but the majority of the Galatian proper names and word endings are Celtic. See Lightfoot, *Com.,* Excursus I. In the controversy as to the Germanic or Celtic nationality of the Galatians, the advocates of the Celtic origin have the best of the argument. More accurately speaking, they were, as indicated above, *prevailingly* Celtic, with a slight mixture of Teutons. So the Celtic French and Irish are mixed with some Teutonic and Norman blood, while the Scotch are more Teutonic (Anglo-Saxon) than Celtic or Gaelic. Luther first hinted at the Germanic origin of the Galatians, and reads the Germans of his day a lesson for their inconstancy and fickleness in the cause of the Reformation. But this fault is rather characteristic of the Gauls, as described by the ancients and confirmed by history.

[3] Hence the name *Gallo-Græci* and *Gallo-Græcia.*

[4] According to Jerome (d. 419), who was a good linguist and spent some time both at Treves and afterwards in Galatia. His testimony that the native tongue of the Galatians was 'almost identical with that of the Treveri' (Introd. to his *Com. on Galat.*) is the chief argument in favor of the Germanic origin of the Galatians advocated by Wieseler and others. But to the Greek and Roman writers the German and the Celtic languages were alike barbarous and unknown, and it is quite probable that

a hundred years of warlike independence they were forced to acknowledge the sovereignty of the Romans (B. C. 187), and their country was finally made a province of the empire under Augustus (B. C. 25).

The principal cities of the province were Ancyra (declared the capital by Augustus), Tavium, and Pessinus. Their commerce attracted many Jews. Ancyra was famous for its goat's-hair manufactures, and for the great historical marble tablets which Augustus had erected there. Pessinus was the centre of the gorgeous and sensuous Phrygian worship of Cybele, the goddess of the earth. In these places were, no doubt, the most important of the congregations to which the Epistle is addressed.

The Galatians were the first of the Celtic and Germanic races to whom the gospel was preached. They are described by the ancient writers as a frank, warlike, impetuous, intelligent, and impressible, but unsteady, quarrelsome, vain, and ostentatious people. It is astonishing how national traits perpetuate themselves for centuries. In both their good and bad qualities and 'the fatal gift of fascination' the ancient Galatians and Gauls strongly resemble the modern French.

Under this generous, impulsive, but changeable character the Galatians appear in the Epistle of St. Paul. They received him first with enthusiastic joy and kindness, but suffered themselves soon to be misled by false teachers.[1] They were, like all the Celts, 'excessive in their devotion to external observances' (as Cæsar describes them). Their former religion was a gross superstition, with a wild, mystic ceremonial, hideous mutilations, revolting cruelty, and slavish obedience to priestly authority. They were emancipated from this bondage by Paul, but as quickly fell away from his pure and spiritual teaching, and embraced another showy, ceremonial, and hierarchical religion, which resembled their old notions and habits. They exchanged a heathen form of ritualism for a Judaizing form, and returned to the 'weak and beggarly elements' and a new 'yoke of bondage.' In the second and third centuries Galatia was a hot-bed of Gnostic heresies and Montanist fanaticism. Gregory of Nazianzen denounces 'the folly of the Galatians, who abound in many impious sects.'

§ 2. Conversion of the Galatians.

St. Paul came first to Galatia during his second great missionary journey, about the year 51, accompanied by Silas and Timothy, and planted the seed of Christianity throughout the province. (Acts xvi. 6; comp. Gal. i. 6–8; iv. 4–13 ff.) He was at that time suffering from bodily infirmity (Gal. iv. 13), in consequence of much fatigue, persecution, manual labor for his support, and that mysterious affliction which he calls a 'thorn in the flesh' (2 Cor. xii. 7). But the grace of God dwelling in him overcame all these obstacles, and revealed its own purity and power all the more strikingly by its contrast with the weakness of nature. The excitable hearts of the Galatians were carried away. They received the Apostle who manifested such zeal and devotion in spite of sickness and pain, as an angel of God, yea, even as Jesus Christ himself, and felt so grateful and happy that they were ready, if possible, to sacrifice their own eyes for the good of the Apostle and the unspeakable gift of the gospel (Gal. iv. 14, 15). This enthusiastic devotion must have

---

both were spoken on the Rhine, and to some extent in Galatia, if the emigration was mixed. Half a century before Jerome visited Treves a colony of German Franks had settled in the neighborhood and gradually displaced the Celtic language, but this must have required a good many years.

[1] So the Reformation started with the fairest prospects in France, and ascended the throne in the person of Henry IV., but was almost crushed out of existence under Louis XIV.

been one of his most cheering experiences Hence, also, his deep grief when he heard soon afterwards of their apostasy to a false gospel.

On his third great missionary journey (A. D. 54 or 55) Paul paid a second visit to Galatia, and confirmed the congregations in the Christian faith (Acts xviii. 23).

The majority of these congregations were, no doubt, converts from heathenism. This appears from chap. iv. 8, 9, where their former condition is described as one of ignorance concerning God, and as a service of false or unreal gods; also from the remark (vi. 12), that the Judaizing errorists constrained them to be circumcised, which implies that they were not circumcised before. (Compare i. 16; ii. 9; iv. 12; v. 23; vi. 12, 13.)

At the same time a number of Galatian converts were originally Jews. This appears from Gal. ii. 15 ff.; iii. 13, 23-25; iv. 3, where the apostle, as a *Jewish* Christian, speaks of himself and his readers in a common plural. This explains the frequent allusions of the Epistle to the Old Testament, and the allegorical interpretation of Sara and Hagar (chap. iv. 21-31). According to Josephus, the Jews were numerous in Ancyra.

The congregations of Galatia were, therefore, like all the churches founded by Paul, of a mixed, yet predominantly Gentile-Christian character. It was his practice to preach the gospel first in the synagogue, and then to the Gentiles, whom he reached through the medium of 'the proselytes of the gate,' *i. e.*, the 'God-fearing' Gentiles or uncircumcised semi-Jews; for these frequently attended the Jewish worship, adopted the monotheism and the Messianic hopes, and were unconsciously in search of Christianity, groping in the dark after the 'unknown God,' whom Paul preached.

The visit of St. Paul to Britain is a pious fancy based on an erroneous interpretation of the 'end of the West,' which he reached in his missionary tours, according to Clement of Rome, but which must either be Rome or Spain (comp. Rom. xv. 24). It is not impossible, however, as Dr. Lightfoot suggests, that some of Paul's Galatian converts, visiting the far West to barter the hair-cloths of their native land, may have first preached the gospel to the Britons in their kindred language. Yet it is more likely that Christianity reached Britain first from the nearer Gaul and Italy in the second century.

§ 3. *Occasion of the Epistle.*

The Epistle was occasioned by the agitations of the Judaizing legalists and formalists, who taught the necessity of circumcision for salvation (v. 2, 11, 12; vi. 12 ff.), and assailed the apostolic authority of Paul, the great champion of the doctrine of salvation by free grace without the works of the law (i. 1, 11; ii. 14). They maintained that he lacked at least one essential qualification for an apostle, having never enjoyed the personal intercourse of Christ on earth, and that he stood in an anomalous position, outside of the regular college of the original twelve. They probably called in question the sincerity of his conversion, and could not forget that he was once a savage persecutor. They regarded him as a dangerous radical and revolutionist, who upset the divinely revealed law and endangered the purity and order of the Church.[1] Their Christianity was in all its essential features identical with the Jewish system, except the belief in the Messiahship of Jesus.

[1] This animosity against Paul was perpetuated among the Ebionites, a Judaizing Christian sect of the early Church. Among modern sects the Swedenborgians have a strong prejudice against Paul, and reject his epistles.

It was simply an improvement of the law of Moses. It could never have converted the world. It would have excluded the noblest of the Gentiles and included the meanest of the Jews. But their error fell in very naturally with the hereditary prejudices of the Jewish converts, especially those of the strict Pharisaic school. They appealed with great apparent force to the letter of the Old Testament, which enjoins circumcision unconditionally upon all male members of Israel; to the practice of the Christian congregation at Jerusalem, which adhered to the Mosaic ritual as long as the congregation consisted exclusively of converted Jews; and to the authority of Peter and James, who, however, had taken more liberal ground since the vision at Joppa and the conversion of Cornelius (Acts x. and xi).

These errorists were defeated in the Council of Jerusalem (Acts xv.), which had decided that faith in Jesus Christ was sufficient for salvation, but they were not convinced, and continued their mischievous work in nearly all the congregations of Paul. They followed him step by step, and tried to undermine his authority and influence. They sneaked into his folds during his absence, and intimidated his defenseless sheep. They reaped where they had not sown. In Galatia they were particularly bold, and succeeded so well among the inexperienced converts that the majority of them for the time being fell away from the liberty of the gospel to the bondage of the law, and ended in the flesh after having begun in the Spirit. Their ceremonial worship captivated the Celtic imagination and emotional temperament more than the spiritual simplicity of Paul's rational service. They told the Galatians that they were only half converted; that they did not yet belong to the church of the true apostolic succession, and had not received the full title-deed to salvation; that they must be circumcised and observe the whole Mosaic law in order to insure their salvation. (Comp. i. 6; iii. 1, 3; iv. 9, 21; v. 2, 7.)

The apostasy took place shortly after the second visit of Paul in Galatia (i. 6, 'I marvel that you are *so soon* removed'). But the false teachers had probably begun their agitation before, since passages like i. 9; v. 3; iv. 16, seem to allude to previous *personal* warnings of the Apostle against the same error.

We need not be surprised in the least at these disturbances. The same spirit of bigotry and exclusiveness reappears again and again in various forms. Sometimes it insists on a particular dogma, at other times on a form of government, or mode of worship, or a particular rite and ceremony, as being necessary to salvation. It springs from the selfishness of the human heart, which would like all other people to conform to us rather than that we should conform to them, or let them have their own ways and work out their own mission. This intolerant spirit is responsible for all the religious persecutions which form the darkest chapter in the history of Christianity, and which are by no means confined to one church or sect. Nearly every sect has at one time of its history been persecuting according to the extent of its power and opportunity. We must all the more be thankful to the great Apostle of the Gentiles for his bold and noble defense of the gospel of freedom.

§ 4. *Object and Contents.*

The object of the Epistle, accordingly, was both apologetic and polemic. It is a personal and a doctrinal self-defense, and a refutation of the Judaizing heresy which had to be once for all uprooted. To this are added appropriate exhortations. The address and salutation, with some remarks on the Galatian defection (i. 1–6), introduces the discussion, and an autographic exhortation and benediction concludes it.

The first part (i. 1 to ii. 14 or 21) is HISTORICAL and PERSONAL, or AUTOBIO-
GRAPHICAL, giving a *résumé* of the Apostle's career, partly confirmatory, partly
supplementary to the narrative of the Acts (chap. xv.), and justifying his office
and authority from the direct call of Christ, the revelation of the gospel doctrine
made to him, and the testimony of the other Apostles during the Council of Jerusalem.

The second part is DOCTRINAL and POLEMICAL (chap. ii. 15 to iv. 31). Others
begin the second part with chap. iii. 1. Paul vindicates and expounds the free
gospel salvation by a living faith in Christ, in opposition to the slavish and carnal
legalism and ceremonialism of the false teachers who would virtually substitute
Moses for Christ.

The third part is PRACTICAL or HORTATORY (chaps. v. and vi.). Paul urges the
Galatians to hold fast to the Christian liberty, yet without abusing it, to study love,
unity, humility, forbearance, and concludes with a benediction.

The main divisions are clear enough. Yet the Epistle is so lively and fervent
that narrative, argument, and exhortation are to some extent blended together.

We do not know the effect of the Epistle upon the Galatians. Paul never visited
them again, but his thoughts and words still live and burn throughout Christendom.

§ 5. *Time and Place of Composition.*

The Epistle must have been written after the Apostolic Council, A. D. 50, since
this is alluded to in chapter ii. 1 ff., and after the year 51, when Paul paid his
first visit to Galatia (Acts xvi. 6). The passage (Gal. iv. 13), 'Ye know how
through infirmity of the flesh I preached the gospel unto you at the first' (former
time), points to a still later date, as it seems to presuppose a second personal visit,
the one mentioned in Acts xviii. 23, which took place A. D. 54 or 55.

On the other hand, however, the words 'so soon' (i. 6) forbid us to bring the
composition down much later than 56.

To the same result we are led by a comparison of Galatians with Second Corinthians and Romans, which bear such a strong resemblance that they must be
assigned to the same period in the life of Paul. The Second Epistle to the Corinthians reveals a similar commotion of feeling, and was written from Macedonia,
on the way to Corinth, in the summer of 57 ; the Epistle to the Romans discusses
the same doctrines, but more calmly, fully, and maturely, and we know it to have
been composed at Corinth shortly before his last journey to Jerusalem, early in the
year 58. Consequently, we may with some degree of certainty place Galatians in
the year 56 or 57, either before or shortly after Second Corinthians, at all events
before Romans. (Comp. § 6.)

As to the *place* of writing, we are pointed either to Ephesus, whither Paul proceeded after his second visit to Galatia, and where he tarried nearly three years,
from 54–57 (Acts xix. 1–10), or to Corinth, where he spent part of the winter
from 57 to 58, or (with Lightfoot and Sanday) to some place on the journey from
Macedonia to Corinth. Ephesus is preferable, as Paul had more time there and
was nearer the Galatians. At all events, the Epistle was written soon after the
apostasy and under the first fresh impressions of the sad news.[1]

---

[1] The common subscription, 'written from *Rome*' (in our English version), which is no part of the
original text, cannot be supported by any external or internal argument, and has, therefore, long
since been given up by the best commentators as the mistake of a transcriber.

§ 6. *The Character and Value of the Epistle.*

The Epistle to the Galatians is the Magna Charta and bulwark of evangelical liberty against all forms of ancient and modern legalism, ceremonialism, and traditionalism. It is a declaration of independence, 'written in jets of flame,' a manifesto of emancipation from the yoke of spiritual bondage. It is a mighty plea for the doctrine of the free grace of God in Christ Jesus, as the only and all-sufficient ground of our salvation; of justification by faith in distinction from all external works and rites; and of the direct relation of the believer to Christ without intervening obstacles. Tertullian, who had something of the bold and fervid spirit of Paul, calls Galatians 'the principal Epistle against Judaism.'

Our Epistle was written in the agony of battle, and smells of powder. It burns with holy indignation, not against the persons of his opponents, whom he never mentions by name, but against their false doctrine and mean, intriguing conduct. It is impetuous and overpowering, and yet affectionate and warning in tone. It strikes like lightning every projecting point that approaches its path, and yet, undelayed by these zigzag deflections, instantaneously attains the goal. Every verse breathes the spirit of the great and free Apostle of the Gentiles. His earnestness and mildness, his severity and love, his vehemence and tenderness, his depth and simplicity, his commanding authority and sincere humility, are here vividly brought before us in fresh and bold outlines. How severe and intimidating is the anathema (i. 8, 9), how sharp and cutting the reproof (iii. 1–4)! But nothing, on the other hand, can be more touchingly affectionate than his reference to the love and gratitude which the Galatians bore to him (iv. 12–15), and the assurance of his anxiety to be present with his 'little children,' of whom he says he was again in travail until Christ be formed in them (iv. 18–20).

The Epistle to the Galatians, as already remarked, bears a striking resemblance to the Epistle to the Romans, not only in particular passages, but in the whole scope and tenor.[1] No two Epistles of Paul are so much alike except Ephesians and Colossians. Both discuss the same doctrines of sin and grace, of the law and the gospel, of the free salvation of Christ, of justification by faith without works. But they differ in the mode of treatment and the state of mind from which they proceed. Galatians is a rapid sketch, a fresh and fervent emotional utterance of those great truths in their bold elementary outlines; Romans is a calm and systematic elaboration of the same truths. The former is all aglow with polemic fervor and personal sympathy; the latter is composed in a serene and peaceful frame of mind, and is free of censure and complaint, since Paul had at that time no personal knowledge of the Roman Christians and could not call them his children. Galatians may be compared to a fierce mountain torrent in continuous rush over the precipices; Romans to a majestic river in a boundless prairie. 'To the Galatians' (says Bishop Lightfoot) 'the Apostle flashes out in indignant remonstrance the first eager thoughts kindled by the zeal for the gospel, striking suddenly against a stubborn form of Judaism. To the Romans he writes at leisure, under no pressure of circumstances, in the face of no direct antagonism, explaining, completing, extending the teaching of the earlier letter, by giving it a double edge directed against

---

[1] Comp. Gal. iii. 6–12 with Rom. iv. 3, 10, 11, 17, 23; iii. 21: Gal. iii. 22 with Rom. xi. 32: Gal. iv. 5, 6, 7 with Rom. viii. 14–17: Gal. ii. 16 with Rom. iii. 20: Gal. ii. 19 with Rom. vi. 8, 11: Gal. v. 14 with Rom. xiii. 8–10: Gal. v. 16 with Rom. viii. 4: Gal. v. 17 with Rom. vii. 23, 25: Gal. vi. 1 with Rom. xv. 1.

Jew and Gentile alike. The matter which in the one Epistle is personal and frag-
mentary, elicited by the special needs of an individual church, is in the other gen-
eralized and arranged so as to form a comprehensive and systematic treatise.'

It is remarkable that these two most evangelical Epistles should have been written to the representatives of those races — the Latin and the Celtic — which have
shown the strongest bent towards that Judaizing type of Christianity which is
therein condemned and refuted.

Our Epistle resembles also the Second Epistle to the Corinthians, not in the subject treated of, but in the intense personality, in the excited state of feeling, the
deep commotion of heart, and the polemic tone towards the false apostles.[1] This
similarity was already observed by a commentator in the fifth century ('Theodore of
Mopsueste), and has been well expressed by a modern commentator (Dr. Jewett)
in these words: 'In both Epistles there is the same sensitiveness in the Apostle to
the behavior of his converts to himself, the same earnestness about the points of
difference, the same remembrance of his "infirmity" while he was yet with them,
the same consciousness of the precarious basis on which his own authority rested
in the existing state of the two churches. In both there is a greater display of his
own feelings than in any other portion of his writings, a deeper contrast of inward
exaltation and outward suffering, more of personal entreaty, a greater readiness to
impart himself.'

The doctrinal meaning and significance of the Epistle to the Galatians, as well
as that of the Epistle to the Romans, was not fully appreciated till the time of the
Reformation. In the hands of Luther and Calvin it became a powerful weapon
against the Judaizers of their age, who wished to entangle the Church again in the
yoke of bondage, and who made salvation depend upon all sorts of outward observances rather than a living faith in Jesus Christ.[2]

In this Epistle we have to this day the divine right and divine seal of genuine
evangelical Protestantism against Romanism as far as this is a revival of Judaism,
and denies to the Christian man that liberty 'wherewith Christ hath made us free.'
But it is also, at the same time, an earnest protest against all pseudo-Protestant-
ism, that would abuse the evangelical freedom and pervert it into antinomian licen-
tiousness, which is the worst kind of slavery. For only

> 'He is a freeman whom the Truth makes free,
> And all are slaves beside.'

§ 7. *Genuineness.*

The external or historical evidence for the Pauline authorship of this Epistle is
not so strong as the evidence for the genuineness of the Gospels, because it was

---

[1] Comp. Gal. i. 6–9 with 2 Cor. ix. 3–7: Gal. ii. 6 with 2 Cor. xii. 11: Gal. ii. 20 with 2 Cor. v. 15:
Gal. iv. 13, 14 with 2 Cor. xii. 7–9: Gal. iv. 17 with 2 Cor. xi. 2: Gal. v. 15 with 2 Cor. xi. 20: Gal.
v. 20, 21 with 2 Cor. xii. 20, 21: Gal. vi. 1 with 2 Cor. ii. 7: Gal. vi. 4 with 2 Cor. xiii. 5: Gal. vi. 8
with 2 Cor. ix. 6: Gal. vi. 15 with 2 Cor. v. 17.

[2] Luther, who in his genius and experience was more Pauline than any of the fathers and reformers
(not excepting Tertullian and Augustine), prized Galatians above all other epistles, and called it his
Catharina von Bora. 'The Epistle to the Galatians,' he says, 'is *my* Epistle. I have betrothed myself to it: it is my wife.' His commentary on Galatians is one of his best works, but it is not
so much an exposition as a free expansion and polemical application of its ideas to the errors of his
day, especially the Anabaptists and the legalism of the Roman church. It also reveals by contrast
the great superiority of an inspired apostle over an enlightened teacher. St. Paul never indulges in
personalities, and his polemic zeal never degenerates into ferocity and coarseness.

less frequently used. The allusions to it in the writings of the Apostolic Fathers at the close of the first and beginning of the second centuries are somewhat indefinite and uncertain. But after the middle of the second century it is freely quoted by Irenæus, Clement of Alexandria, Tertullian, and other fathers. All the manuscripts and versions ascribe it to St. Paul; and Eusebius counts it among the homologoumena, or the universally recognized books of the New Testament. It was also used by early heretics, especially by the Gnostic Marcion (about 150), who included it in his canon as the first of Paul's Epistles, and made it (like the Tübingen Gnostics) the chief basis of his protest against what he regarded as the Judaizing books of the New Testament.

The internal evidence for the authorship of Paul is so strong that no sane divine has ever denied or even doubted it. If there is any genuine document of Paulinism in existence, it is the Epistle to the Galatians. Its marked individuality places it beyond the reach of imitation. It is as unmistakable as the Lutheranism of Luther's commentary on it. The thoughts and style of the Epistle from beginning to end are thoroughly characteristic of Paul, and in full harmony with all we know about his life and doctrine and the history of the apostolic age. There is no man in the early church who could have written such an original, vigorous, profound, and authoritative vindication of the gospel of freedom against Judaizing error but the great Apostle of the Gentiles, whose name it bears, and of whose personality it is a full-length portrait.[1]

---

[1] It was left to a half-crazy hypercritic of the nineteenth century (Bruno Bauer, *Kritik der Paulin. Briefe*, 1850) to stultify himself by declaring that the Epistle to the Galatians is a confused compilation from the Epistles to the Romans and Corinthians. His arguments are not worth refuting. Dr. F. Chr. Baur, of Tübingen (d. 1860), the boldest and most learned of modern skeptics, left the Galatians, together with the Romans and Corinthians, untouched, as being beyond all controversy genuine productions of the Apostle Paul.

CHAPTER I.

Address and Greeting.

CHAPTER I. 1-5.

The very address reveals the occasion of the Epistle, the commotion and fervor of Paul, and the
weightiness of his subject : (1) by the emphasis laid on his independent apostolic office and dignity,
which had been called in question by the Judaizing errorists ; (2) by the reference to the atoning death
of Christ, which the Galatians practically undervalued in their legalistic tendency ; and (3) by the
doxology (ver. 5), which indicates his fervent zeal for the glory of God in opposition to every over
valuation of human works.

1 PAUL, an Apostle (*a* not of men, neither by man, but *b* by Jesus Christ,[1] and God the Father, *c* who raised him from
2 the dead),[2] and all *d* the brethren which [3] are with me, *e* unto the churches [4] of Galatia : [5]
3 *f* Grace *be* [6] to you, and peace, from God the Father, and *from* [7]
4 our Lord Jesus Christ, *g* who gave himself for our sins, that he might deliver us *h* from [8] this [9] present evil world,[10] according to
5 the will of God and our Father,[11] *i* to whom *be* glory [12] for ever and ever.[13] Amen.

a Ver. 11, 12.
b Acts ix. 6;
  xx. 24; 1
  Tim. i. 1;
  Tit. i. 3.
c Acts ii. 24.
d Phil. iv. 21.
e 1 Cor. xvi. 1.
f Rom. i. 7;
  1 Cor. i. 3.
g Matt. xx.
  28; Rom. iv.
  14.
h John xv.
  19; xvii. 14;
  1 John v. 19.
i Rom. xi. 36.

[1] not from men, nor through man, but through Jesus Christ
[2] *omit parenthesis*   [3] who   [4] *or* congregations
[5] *put period after* Galatia, *and begin a new sentence with* Grace
[6] *omit* be   [7] *omit* from   [8] out of   [9] the
[10] *Lit.,* age   [11] *or,* our God and Father   [12] *is* the glory
[13] *Lit.,* unto the ages of the ages

Ver. 1 contains the text of the first two chapters : namely, the divine mission and independent
apostolic authority of Paul, which the Judaizers
denied, but which is clearly proved by the following narrative and the testimony of the older Apostles themselves. Ver. 4 implies the theme of the
second part, chaps. iii. and iv., namely, a defense
of the doctrine of free grace in Christ. — **An Apostle,** lit., *messenger ;* here in the highest sense : one
of the special messengers of Christ and witnesses
of his resurrection who were (1) *directly* called by
him, (2) *inspired* by the Holy Spirit, and hence
infallible in their religious teaching, and (3) commissioned to *all* nations ; hence the founders and
authoritative teachers of the whole church in all
ages. See note on Rom. i. 1. The Judaizers
confined the apostolic dignity to the Twelve, to

whom Paul did not belong. He represented the
independent apostolate of the Gentiles. — **Not
from men, nor through man.** Paul's apostleship
is entirely independent of human agency, direct
or indirect. The preposition ' from ' denotes the
origin or fountain, the preposition ' through ' the
instrumentality or channel. The singular ' through
man ' (any man whatever) makes the exclusion of
human agency stronger, and forms a contrast to
the following **through Jesus Christ,** who is more
than a man. ' Through ' includes here for brevity's sake both the nearer instrumental and the
more remote originating source of authority. Paul
was called at his conversion on the way to Damascus, when the risen and ascended Saviour
appeared to him personally (Acts ix. 15). The
Apostles are both ' from Christ ' and ' through

Christ;' their disciples (and all regular teachers of the church) are 'from' Christ, but 'through man;' the false teachers are 'from men' and 'through man,' or self-constituted intruders without any authority from Christ. Paul's call was just as direct as that of the Twelve; but the Judaizers, in their tendency to overrate external forms and secondary causes, laid great stress upon the personal intercourse with Christ in the days of his flesh, and hence they were disposed either to declare Paul a pseudo-apostle, or at least to subordinate him to the Twelve, especially to Peter and James. — **And God the Father.** The immediate and frequent coördination of Christ with God the Father, especially here in contrast with the preceding *men* and *man*, proves that the Apostle regarded the Saviour as a Divine being. God is the Father, not indiscriminately of all men (though He is the creator, preserver, and judge of all), but of Christ, His only begotten and eternal Son, and of all believers who by regeneration become the children of God (iv. 6; Rom. viii. 15; John i. 13). God is 'our' Father, because He is the Father (not simply of 'Jesus Christ,' which would place Christ on a par with us, but) of '*our Lord* Jesus Christ' (comp. Rom. xv. 6; 2 Cor. i. 3; xi. 31; Eph. i. 3; iii. 14; I Pet. i. 3). — **Who raised him from the dead.** It was the *risen* Saviour who called Paul to the apostleship, who founded the Church and gave some Apostles, some prophets, and some evangelists (comp. Eph. iv. 11).

Ver. 2. **And all the brethren who are with me.** The companions and co-laborers of Paul, such as Silas, Timothy, Luke, Sosthenes, some of whom are expressly mentioned in the address of other Epistles (1 Cor. i. 1; 2 Cor. i. 1; Phil. i. 1; I Thess. i. 1; 2 Thess. ii. 1). The word 'all' seems to imply a considerable number. The reason why he mentions others is his strong sense of brotherly communion, rather than the desire to give additional force to his exhortations. — **Unto the churches of Galatia.** In Ancyra, Pessinus, Tavium, and other towns of the province. 'Churches' are here (as often) local congregations, which belong to the church universal. In the New Testament the word 'church' has only two senses: (1) the whole church; (2) a particular congregation. We use it in two additional senses: (3) a confession or denomination (the Roman, the Anglican, the Lutheran, Church, etc.); (4) a church building. The Epistle was encyclical, or intended for several congregations, like the Epistle to the Hebrews and that to the Ephesians. Hence the absence of individual greetings at the close. The mere mention of the name without those honorable epithets (as 'saints in Christ,' 'faithful brethren') which he bestows upon other congregations, betrays his dissatisfaction with the apostate Galatians. He has no words of praise for them; they must be chastised like disobedient and ungrateful children.

Ver. 3. **Grace to you and peace.** The apostolic salutation combines the Greek *charis* ('grace') and the Hebrew *shalom* ('peace'), and infuses into both a deep Christian meaning. 'Grace' comprehends the fulness of the gospel blessing, 'peace' the fulness of our personal enjoyment of it and happiness resulting from it. — **From God the Father, and our Lord Jesus Christ.** The Father is the direct giver, the Son the mediator, of saving grace and inward peace; but both are here (as in ver. 1) so immediately associated that

we have a right to infer from this the divinity of our Lord. No mere man could, without blasphemy, be put into such juxtaposition with the infinite Jehovah as a giver of grace and peace.

Ver. 3 forms a sentence for itself, distinct from the address or inscription in vers. 1 and 2 (comp. note on Rom. i. 7). Some ancient authorities read 'from God our Father and the Lord Jesus Christ.'

Ver. 4. Paul here touches on the doctrinal, as in ver. 1 he touched on the personal, point of controversy with the false teachers. He holds up at once before the Galatians, who were returning to the bondage of the law, the picture of the dying Saviour, who, by the one sacrifice on the cross, fully and forever accomplished our redemption, so that we need not resort to any human means of salvation or go back to a preparatory dispensation. — **Who gave himself,** nothing less than His own person, into death, as a ransom and expiatory sacrifice (Rom. iv. 25; 1 Tim. ii. 6; Tit. ii. 14; Matt. xx. 28). — **For our sins,** to atone for them, and thereby to abolish the guilt and to reconcile us to God (Rom. iii. 25; Gal. iii. 13). All sins are included, great and small, past and present, known and unknown. — **That he might deliver us.** Lit., *tear away*, from a power, the expression used by the Lord of Paul's own deliverance (Acts xxvi. 17). 'It strikes the key-note of the Epistle. The gospel is a rescue, an emancipation from a state of bondage' (Lightfoot). — **From** (or **out of**) **this present evil world** (æon, age), from the state and order of this transitory world, where sin and death reign, from the world which lies in wickedness (1 John v. 19), in opposition to the supernatural order of the heavenly kingdom, which begins even here on earth (for he who believeth in Christ '*hath* eternal life'), but which will not be fully revealed till the glorious appearance of Christ (Rom. xii. 2; Eph. ii. 2; 1 Tim. vi. 17; Heb. vi. 5). The words contain an allusion to the Jewish distinction between 'this world' and 'the world to come,' or the period before and the period after the appearance of the Messiah. But the distinction is modified in the New Testament: the present world of temptation and trial extends to the second and glorious coming of Christ; and the future world, though beginning here in faith, does not fully appear to sight till the consummation. The primary distinction of time (present and future) is lost in the moral distinction (good and evil); and hence 'evil' is placed in the Greek emphatically at the end. The verse implies a longing after the glorious liberty of the children of God. The Apostles lived on the border line of two æons, looking sadly on one and hopefully on the other. So all true Christians are pilgrims and strangers in this world of sin and sorrow, and have their citizenship in heaven. — **According to the will of God,** from whom the whole plan and process of redemption proceeds, so that all the glory belongs to Him, and not to man. The sacrifice of the Son was not forced, or even commanded, by the Father, but strictly voluntary, as is implied in the preceding words: 'Who gave himself for our sins' (comp. John x. 18). It was the act of His free love in full harmony with the eternal design of the Father, who 'is not desiring that any should perish, but that all should come unto repentance' (2 Peter iii. 9). — **And our Father,** who is at the same time our loving, merciful Father, and who out of infinite love gave His Son for our salvation.

Our,' however, may also be connected with both nouns: 'our God and Father.'

Ver. 5. **To whom** (*is*) **the glory**, without diminution or division. The article denotes that it is the glory which essentially belongs to God, and to God alone. To boundless mercy belongs boundless praise and gratitude. It is an affirmation (*is*) rather than a wish (*be*); comp. Matt vi. 13; 1 Pet. iv. 11. The doxology in this place implies an indirect reproof of the Galatians for dividing the glory of our salvation between God and man.

Similar doxologies, flowing from an overwhelming sense of gratitude, are frequent with Paul, in connection with the mention of the Christian salvation (Rom. xi. 36; xvi. 26; Eph. iii. 21; Phil. iv. 20; 2 Tim. iv. 18). — **For ever and ever**, lit., '*unto the ages of ages*' (*æons of æons, sæcula sæculorum*), — a Hebraizing term for very long, or (as here) endless duration. In opposition to the present transitory world (ver. 4; comp. Eph. ii. 2, 7).

The Apostasy of the Galatians; Anathema on the False Teachers.

CHAPTER I. 6–10.

In all other Epistles Paul begins in a spirit of Christian courtesy and love, thanksgiving and encouragement, thereby winning the affections and securing the respectful attention of his readers. But here he begins with an indignant expression of his painful surprise at the speedy apostasy of his spiritual children, and enters his solemn protest against every perversion of the gospel of Christ, whom alone he served in his ministry. Yet his deep emotion is more that of sorrow than of anger, and implies his profound interest in the Galatians (comp. iv. 19). He chastises them in order to win them back to their former position. It was his love that made him severe.

6 I MARVEL that ye are so soon removed [1] from *a* him that *a* Chap. v. 8.
   called you into [2] the grace of Christ [3] unto another [4] gospel, *b* 2 Cor. xi. 4;
   comp. Acts
7 *b* which is not another; but there be some [5] *c* that trouble you, iv. 17;
   c Chap. v. 10,
8 and would pervert the gospel of Christ. But though we, [6] or *d* an 12; Acts xv.
   1, 24; 2 Cor.
   angel from heaven, preach [7] any other gospel unto you [8] than xi. 13.
   d 2 Cor. xi.
   that [9] which we have preached unto you *e* let him be accursed. [10] *e* Deut. iv. 2;
9 As we said before, so say I now again, If any *man* preach any xii. 13.
   Prov. xxx.
   other gospel unto you than that ye have received, *e* let him be 6; Rev.
   xxii. 18.
10 accursed. [10]   For do I now persuade men, [11] or God? or *f* do I *f* 1 Thess. ii.
    4; comp.
    seek [12] to please men? For if I yet pleased men, [13] I should Rom. ii. 29;
    1 Cor. x. 33;
    not be the servant [14] of Christ. Eph. vi. 6;
    Col. iii. 22.

[1] so quickly turning away, *or* removing   [2] in
[3] *make a comma after* Christ   [4] a different
[5] save (except) that there are some   [6] even though we (*or*, I myself)
[7] should preach   [8] *some ancient authorities omit* unto you
[9] any gospel unto you beside that (*or*, contrary to that). *So also ver.* 9.
[10] anathema
[11] For am I now persuading (winning over) men (*or*, am I now seeking the favor of men)   [12] am I seeking (striving)
[13] if I were still pleasing men   [14] a bondman

Ver. 6. **I marvel.** A sharp rebuke in a mild word, which challenges explanation, and intimates that better things were expected from the Galatians. — **So quickly**, namely, either after your conversion, which is alluded to in 'who called you,' or after my second and last visit to you, or after the arrival of the false teachers. The first is the most probable. In any case the word points to an early date of the Epistle. (See Introd., § 5.) Even the best preaching cannot prevent apostasy.

Grotius cites in illustration of the Galatian character what Cæsar says of the Gauls (the ancestors of the French): 'They are quick and resolute, and fond of change and novelties.' — **Turning away**; *changing over*; here and often in a bad sense, *turning renegades, deserters.* The Greek (middle voice) implies first that the apostasy was voluntary on their part, and hence their own guilt; secondly, that it was not yet completed, but still in progress, and hence might be arrested. (The passive rendering of the Latin Vulgate and English Version would transfer the guilt to the false teachers, and soften the censure of the Galatians.) — **From him**, not Paul, but God the Father, from whom the gospel call always proceeds (comp. i. 15; 1 Cor. i. 9; vii. 15, 17; Rom. viii. 30; ix. 11, 24; 1 Thess. ii. 12; 2 Thess. ii. 14; 2 Tim. i. 9; 1 Peter i. 15; ii. 9; v. 10).— In (not **into**, as the English Version has it, following the Vulgate) **the grace of Christ**. The grace, *i. e.*, the whole work, of Christ as a manifestation of His redeeming love is both the element *in* which and the medium *by* or *through* which the Father draws to the Son (John vi. 44) and effects the call (comp. Acts xv. 11; Rom. v. 15).— **Unto a different gospel**, different in kind, another sort of gospel, which is undeserving of the name, since there is but one gospel, namely, that to which you were called by God. Hence Paul immediately adds a correction of this paradoxical expression, which he uses simply in accommodation to the language of the Judaizing pseudo-evangelists (comp. 2 Cor. xi. 4).

Ver. 7. **Which** (pseudo-gospel of the heretical teachers) **is not another**, *i. e.*, no gospel at all, but a perversion and corruption of the one unchangeable gospel. The gospel of Paul teaches that man is justified *by grace alone* through faith in Jesus Christ; the pseudo-gospel of the Judaizers teaches that man is justified by grace *and works* through faith in Christ *and the circumcision* of Moses. The former makes good works the effect, the latter the cause, of justification; and this is thus in fact a relapse into the Jewish standpoint under a Christian name.— **Save that there are some troubling you**. Only in this sense is it another gospel that it is a perversion of the true gospel of Christ by those well-known troublers of your conscience.

Ver. 8. **But even though we ourselves** (I and my colleagues, ver. 2), **or an angel from heaven, should preach [unto you] any gospel other than that** (beyond that) **which we preached unto you, let him be anathema**. It is impossible to express more strongly and solemnly the conviction of the unerring truth of the gospel as preached by Paul, the zeal for its purity, and the aversion to every heresy. Only an inspired Apostle could thus speak. The condemnation of the opponents is indirect, but the more certain by the argument *a fortiori*. The severity of Paul against *false* brethren was equalled by his forbearance with *weak* brethren (comp. vi. 1; Rom. xiv. 1 and xv. 1). All personal assumption and arrogance is here excluded, the more so as he conditionally includes himself and his colleagues in the anathema. His only motive was zeal for the purity of the gospel of his divine Lord and Master.— **An angel from heaven**, proverbial expression for a being possessed of the highest authority next to the divine. **Beside that**; lit., *beyond what*, which is both *beside* (*præterea*)

and *against* (*contra*). The gospel admits of no rival, either in the form of foreign additions or in the form of changes. Paul condemns not indeed mere differences in form, such as existed even among the Apostles themselves, and will always exist, but every material alteration of the gospel, either by perversion, or omission, or such additions as contradict the spirit of apostolic teaching. The Judaizers did not expressly deny the doctrine of justification by faith, but they indirectly undermined it by adding the assertion of the coördinate necessity of circumcision; just as the Pharisees professed to hold fast to the Word of God in the Old Testament, and yet made it of none effect by their human traditions (comp. Mark vii. 13). The passage admits of easy application to the unscriptural traditions of the Greek and Roman churches. — **Let him be anathema**, anathematized, *i. e.*, devoted (in a bad sense), given over to the judgment of God. It is a solemn judgment of condemnation as in the name of God (comp. 1 Cor. xvi. 22: 'If any man love not the Lord Jesus Christ, let him be anathema;' also Gal. iii. 13; v. 10; Rom. ix. 3; 1 Cor. xii. 3). Subsequently, among the fathers the idea of ecclesiastical excommunication (accompanied sometimes with an execration) was attached to this term; but this is not the Biblical sense, and in our passage it is forbidden by the mention of an angel who cannot be excommunicated from the church.

Ver. 9. **Before** refers not to ver. 8, which is too near, but to the last visit of Paul to Galatia. — **Preach** (εὐαγγελίζεται) implies the actual fact, not the mere possibility, as the hypothetical **should preach** (εὐαγγελίσηαι, ver. 8), and thus attacks more directly the Galatian pseudo-apostles.

Ver. 10 accounts for, and thus softens, the apparently excessive severity of the preceding condemnation. The service of the gospel is absolutely irreconcilable with the selfish service of men. We should indeed serve our fellow-men (comp. Rom. xv. 1–3), but for God's sake, and for the promotion of his glory.— **Persuading**, trying to conciliate or to gain favor by persuasion. — **Still**, *i. e.*, after my call to the apostleship, and all that has happened to me. This does not necessarily imply that in his former state he was a time-server and pleaser of men, who sought the favor of the Jews when he persecuted the Christians. He was never dishonest or dishonorable. A certain manly independence and fearless regard to duty seems to have characterized him even before his conversion.— **I should not be a servant of Christ** (lit., bondman, slave), as described with such power and beauty, 1 Cor. iv. 9–13; 2 Cor. xi. 23 ff. The Galatian heretics, under the assumed character of servants of Christ, sought not the glory of Christ and the salvation of souls, but only the favor of men and their own profit. The Greek fathers miss the meaning when they explain: I would not have left Judaism and become a Christian.

Apostolical Call and Authority of Paul.

CHAPTER I.   11-24.

Paul now enters upon his apology. He defends first his independent apostolical dignity (ver. 11 to ii. 11), and proves that he was called directly by Christ, that he received his gospel through revelation before he became even acquainted with the older Apostles, and that he was recognized by them in his independent apostleship at the conference of Jerusalem. The several points he makes are these : (1.) I did not learn the gospel from men in my youth ; on the contrary, I was a violent persecutor (vers. 13, 14) ; (2.) I learned it directly from Christ when He revealed Himself to me and called me at my conversion (ver. 15) ; (3.) I was not instructed by men after my conversion, for I retired forthwith into the desert of Arabia where there were no Christians (ver. 17) ; (4.) nor by the Apostles in Jerusalem, for I only saw Peter and James, and them but for a few days (ver. 18) ; (5.) at a later visit to Jerusalem I met the Apostles on equal terms and was fully acknowledged by them (ii. 1-10) ; (6.) I even openly rebuked Peter, at Antioch., for his inconsistency (ii. 11-14).

These allusions to important facts in his former life are of great value for a biography of Paul, and tend partly to confirm, partly to supplement the account of the Acts concerning his conversion, his relation to the other Apostles, and the council of Jerusalem. The differences are such as must be expected from two independent writers and can be easily reconciled.

11 [a]BUT I certify you,[1] brethren, that the gospel which was
12 preached of[2] me is not after[3] man. For [b]I neither received it of man,[4] neither[5] was I taught it, but[6] [c]by the revelation[7] of Jesus Christ.

13 For ye have heard of my conversation in time past in the Jews' religion,[8] how that [d]beyond measure I persecuted the
14 church of God, and [e]wasted it :[9] And profited in the Jews' religion above many my equals in mine own nation,[10] [f]being more exceedingly zealous [g]of[11] the traditions of my fathers.

15 But when it pleased God, [h]who separated me[12] from my
16 mother's womb, and called me by[13] his grace, [i]To reveal his Son in[14] me, that [k]I might preach him among the heathen ;[15]
17 immediately I conferred not[16] with [l]flesh and blood : Neither went I up to Jerusalem to them which[17] were apostles before me ; but I went[18] into Arabia, and returned again unto Damascus.

18 Then after three years [m]I went up to Jerusalem to see
19 Peter,[19] and abode[20] with him fifteen days. But [n]other of the

Marginal references:
a 1 Cor xv. 1.
b Ver. 1; 1 Cor. xv. 1,3. Ver. 16; ii. 2; see 1 Cor.
c ii. 10; 2 Cor. xii. 1; Eph. iii. 3.
d Acts ix. 1; xxii. 4; xxvi. 11; 1 Tim. i. 13.
e Acts viii. 3; ix. 21.
f Acts xxii. 3; xxvi. 9; Phil. iii. 6.
g Jer. ix. 14; Matt. xv. 2; Mark vii. 5.
h Is. xlix. 1, 5; Jer. i. 5; Luke i. 15; Acts ix. 15; xiii. 2; Rom. i. 1.
i See ver. 12.
k Acts ix. 15; xxii. 21; xxvi. 17, 18; Rom. xi. 13; Eph. iii. 8.
l Matt. i. 17; 1 Cor. xv. 50; Eph. vi. 12.
m Acts ix. 26, 27.
n 1 Cor. ix 5

---

[1] Now (according to another reading For) I make known to you   [2] by
[3] according to   [4] neither did I myself receive it from man   [5] nor
[6] it came to me   [7] through revelation
[8] For ye heard of my former manner of life in Judaism
[9] Was destroying it (labored to destroy it)
[10] and made progress in Judaism beyond many of mine own age in my race (nation)
[11] for   [12] set me apart   [13] through   [14] within   [15] Gentiles
[16] held no counsel with   [17] to those who   [18] went away
[19] to make the acquaintance of Cephas   [20] remained

20 apostles saw I none, save [21] ° James the Lord's brother.[22] Now ° Matt. xiii. 55; Mark vi.
the things which [23] I write unto you, *behold, before God, I , Rom. ix. 1.
lie not.

21   *Afterwards [24] I came into the regions of Syria and Cilicia ; q Acts ix. 30.

22 And was [25] unknown by face * unto the churches of Judea which * 1 Thess. ii. 14.

23 *were in Christ: But they had heard only,[26] That he which * Rom. xvi. 7.
persecuted us in times past now preacheth the faith which once

24 he destroyed.[27] And they 'glorified God in me.   t See 1 Pet. ii. 12.

[21] But I saw no other of the Apostles but only
[22] the brother of the Lord   [23] But what (or, as to the things which)
[24] Then   [25] And I was still
[26] but this only they were hearing (had heard)
[27] He who was once persecuting us is now preaching the faith he was once
destroying (laboring to destroy)

Ver. 11. **Now I make known to you.** This verb introduces a deliberate and emphatic statement of opinion (as in 1 Cor. xv. 1; 2 Cor. viii. 1). After the warm burst of feeling he proceeds to calm reasoning. Paul still acknowledges the readers as **brethren,** hoping to win them back from their error. — **According to man.** The gospel in its origin and contents as received and taught by Paul is not human, but divine; yet intended for man, and satisfying the deepest wants of man's nature.

Ver. 12. **For neither did I myself receive it from man, nor was I taught it, but** (it came to me) **through revelation of Jesus Christ.** 'I myself' any more than the older Apostles. The opponents denied the equality of Paul with the original Twelve on that score; hence the 'neither.' 'Receive' signifies the passive, 'taught' the active or coöperative mode of appropriation. The former refers more to historical, the latter to doctrinal knowledge. Paul was man-taught as a rabbinical scholar, but God-taught as a Christian Apostle. — 'Through revelation of (from) Jesus Christ,' especially on the way to Damascus (Acts ix. 3 ff). This was the fundamental and central illumination of Paul, corresponding to the pentecostal inspiration of the Twelve, but it was followed by special revelations at different periods of his life (comp. Gal. ii. 2; Acts xxii. 17; xxiii. 11; 1 Cor. xi. 13; 2 Cor. xii. 1 ff.). He speaks of the abundance of his revelations. We may therefore assume a steady growth of the Apostles in divine knowledge. St. Peter, also, after Pentecost, received the vision at Joppa (Acts x.), which enlightened him concerning the exact relation of the gospel to the Gentiles, and thus marked a progress in his inspired knowledge and in the history of missions. Revelation is distinguished from ordinary illumination and instruction by its divine origin, its elevation above (not against) reason, and its sudden communication and intuitive perception. Paul does not mean here the outward historical information concerning the life of Christ which he could derive in part, at least, from reliable eye-witnesses, but chiefly the internal exhibition of Christ to his spiritual sense in his true character as the Messiah and the only and all-sufficient Saviour of the world, and the unfolding of the true import of his atoning death

and resurrection; in other words, the spiritual communication of the gospel system of saving truth as taught by him in his sermons and Epistles.

Ver. 13. **For ye heard** (when I was with you) **of my former manner of life** (or, conduct) **in Judaism,** i. e., the Jewish religion as opposed to Christianity, the religion of the Jewish hierarchy and the Pharisaic school, not the genuine religion of the Old Testament. Paul appeals to the well-known fact of his past career as a persecutor, which formed a part of his teaching, and conclusively proved that no mere human teaching could have converted him. All his antecedents were of such a character that nothing but a divine intervention could produce so great a change. — **That beyond measure I persecuted the church of God and was destroying it,** or 'labored to destroy it' (the same word as in Acts ix. 21). Paul intended to annihilate Christianity, was actually employed in the attempt and carried it out as far as he could (comp. Acts xxii. 4). 'I persecuted this way (or, belief) *even to death*' (xxvi. 10, 11).

Ver. 14. **And made progress** (or, advanced) **in Judaism beyond many of mine own age in my race** (or, nation), **being more exceedingly zealous for the traditions of my fathers.** Paul far surpassed in zeal for the Jewish religion his contemporary kinsmen or fellow-religionists. He belonged to the extreme party of the Pharisees who called themselves 'zealots of the law, zealots of God'; comp. Acts xxii. 3, 'I was zealous towards God'; xxiii. 6, 'I am a Pharisee, the son of a Pharisee' (Phil. iii. 5, 6). — 'Traditions of my fathers' are the law of Moses with all the explanations and additions of the Pharisees (afterwards embodied in the Mishna), which concealed rather than unveiled the Word of God and either hindered or destroyed its direct effect (comp. Matt. xv. 2; Mark vii. 3, 13). Perhaps the written law is not included here. 'Tradition' (*paradosis*) embraces everything which is handed down orally or in writing from generation to generation. It occurs twelve times in the New Testament, twice in a good sense of the Christian doctrine itself (1 Cor. xi. 2, rendered 'ordinances' in the English version; 2 Thess. ii. 15; iii. 6); in the other passages in an unfavorable sense of the human additions to, and perversions of, the written word of God; hence defined as 'traditions *of the elders*'

(Matt. xv. 2, 3, 6; Mark vii. 3, 5, 8, 9, 13), or 'tradition *of men*' (Col. ii. 8). Our Saviour never appeals to the Jewish traditions except to oppose them; and this is of great moment in the controversy with Romanism, which relies more on ecclesiastical traditions than on the Bible.

Vers. 15, 16. **But when it pleased God who set me apart from my mother's womb, and called me through his grace, to reveal his Son within me,** etc. Now he comes to his conversion and accumulates words to show the sole agency of God and the entire absence of all effort and merit of his own in this radical change from fanatical and persecuting Judaism to the apostleship of Christ. Lightfoot well explains the drift of vers. 15–17: 'Then came my conversion. It was foreordained before I had any separate existence. It was not, therefore, due to any merits of my own. The revelation of His Son in me, the call to preach to the Gentiles, were acts of His pleasure. Thus converted, I took no counsel of human advisers. I did not betake myself to the elder Apostles as I might naturally have done. I secluded myself in Arabia, and, when I emerged from my retirement, instead of going to Jerusalem, I returned to Damascus.' — 'Pleased,' according to His free, sovereign will, uninfluenced by any cause from without. — 'Set me apart,' elected and devoted me to the gospel service; comp. the same word in Rom. i. 1; Acts xiii. 2, and the corresponding Hebrew verb *hiphdil*, which is used of the separation and dedication of the priests and Levites to the service of God (Numb. viii. 14; xvi. 9; 1 Chr. xxiii. 13). The English version 'separated' is misleading. — 'From my mother's womb,' before I was born, or from the moment of my birth and personal existence. The same is said of Isaiah (xlix. 1, 'the Lord hath called me from the womb, from the bowels of my mother hath he made mention of my name'), of Jeremiah (i. 5), and of John the Baptist (Luke i. 15). The decree of election is as eternal as God's omniscience and love (comp. Eph. i. 4), but its actualization in time begins with the natural birth and is completed with the spiritual birth or the effectual call.

Ver. 16. **To reveal** depends on 'pleased,' not on 'called.' — **Within me,** in my inmost soul and consciousness. The external manifestation of the exalted Redeemer from heaven on the way to Damascus was accompanied by an inner illumination. — **That I might preach him among the Gentiles.** The conversion of Paul coincided with his call to the apostleship (Acts xxvi. 16–18), but the latter was also newly revealed or confirmed to him in a vision at Jerusalem (Acts xxii. 17, 21). He usually addressed himself first to the Jews, but this was only the natural and divinely appointed bridge to the mission among the Gentiles. The converted Jews and proselytes of the gate who attended the synagogue worship formed the nucleus of his congregations. — **Immediately I conferred not with** (or, **made no communication to, held no counsel with) flesh and blood.** 'Immediately' (or, 'forthwith,' 'straightway') properly belongs to 'I went away' (ver. 17), the negative clause being interposed; or it may be connected with the whole sentence as expressing a single thought: 'Forthwith, instead of consulting with flesh and blood, and going up to the older Apostles in Jerusalem, I departed to Arabia.' When God calls we must obey at once without asking anybody's advice. — 'Flesh and blood' is a He-

brew term for *man* with the accessory idea of weakness or frailty (comp. Matt. xvi. 17; Eph. vi. 12; Heb. ii. 14). Paul means here not his sinful nature which rebelled against the divine grace, but other weak men; for his object is to prove his entire independence of human instruction and counsel. Ananias did no more than baptize him and lay his hands on him (Acts ix. 15–19).

According to Acts ix. 20, Paul spent '*some* days' at Damascus and preached 'immediately' after his conversion to the Jews in the synagogue; but this was probably only an open confession of his faith in the Messiahship of Jesus. He did not enter upon the active duties of the apostleship till three years later. After his return from Arabia he preached in Damascus more fully and provoked the opposition of the Jews which compelled him to leave; Acts ix. 23 (after '*many* days'); comp. 2 Cor. xi. 32. It is not necessary, therefore, to assume that Luke's 'immediately' is an error of chronology.

Ver. 17. **Neither went I up to Jerusalem.** The usual term, as Jerusalem was not only the religious capital of the Jews,[1] but situated on a high hill so that travellers from the east and the west, the north and the south, have to ascend. — **To those who were apostles before me.** The Twelve, including perhaps also James (comp. ver. 19), who, although not one of them, was enjoying an almost apostolic authority as a brother of Jesus and as the head of the congregation in Jerusalem. Paul concedes to the other Apostles no other preference but the priority of call. He knew and declared in all humility that by the grace of God he labored more in word and deed than they all (1 Cor. xv. 10; 2 Cor. xi. 5, 23). — **But I went away (or, departed) into Arabia.** This visit is not mentioned in the Acts (ix. 23), probably because it had no public importance, but belonged to the inner and private history of Paul. 'It is,' as Lightfoot says, 'a mysterious pause, a moment of suspense in the Apostle's history, a breathless calm which ushers in the tumultuous storm of his active missionary life.' After the great moral revolution which shook his body and soul, he needed repose and time of preparation for his apostleship by prayer, meditation, and the renewed study of the Old Testament, in the light of its fulfilment in the person and work of Jesus of Nazareth.[2] This retreat took the place of the three years' preparation of the older Apostles in the school of Christ. The precise locality is a matter of conjecture and dispute, as 'Arabia' has an indefinite meaning. Some seek it not far from Damascus which is surrounded by desert and is called 'the Eye of the Desert.' Others give the journey a deeper significance by extending it to the Sinaitic Peninsula, which is certainly meant by 'Arabia' in Gal. iv. 25; and this would more easily explain the typical allusion to Mount Sinai in the fourth chapter. 'Here, surrounded by the children of the desert, the descendants of Hagar

---

[1] In England and Scotland people 'go *up* to London,' no matter from what part of the country.

[2] Chrysostom entirely misses the meaning of this journey to Arabia by making it an active mission tour, saying: 'See how fervent was his soul; he was eager to occupy lands yet untilled: he forthwith attacked a barbarous and savage people, choosing a life of conflict and much toil.' There is no trace of Christianity in Arabia at so early a time. Hence Jerome (probably following Origen) understood Arabia allegorically for the Old Testament: 'In the law and the prophets Paul sought Christ, and having found H'm there he returned to Damascus, and then went to Jerusalem, the place of vision and peace.'

the bondwoman, he read the true meaning and power of the law' (Lightfoot). Here Paul could commune with the spirit of Moses the lawgiver, and Elijah the prophet, as Christ had communed with them on the Mount of Transfiguration ; here he could study face to face 'the ministration of death and condemnation,' as he calls the old covenant, on the spot of its birth, and by contrast also 'the ministration of the spirit and righteousness' (2 Cor. iii. 7-9). There is no spot on earth where one may receive a stronger and deeper impression of the terrible majesty of God's law, which threatens death to the transgressor, than on Mount Sinai and the awful panorama of desolation and death which surrounds it. To quote from my own experience : 'Such a sight of terrific grandeur and awful majesty I never saw before, nor expect to see again in this world. At the same time I felt more than ever before the contrast between the old and new dispensations : the severity and terror of the law, and the sweetness and loveliness of the gospel' (Schaff, *Through Bible Lands*, p. 172).—**And returned again unto Damascus.** The place of his conversion, one of the oldest and most interesting cities in the world, known in the days of Abraham (Gen. xiv. 15 ; xv. 2), conquered by David (2 Sam. viii. 5, 6), and after various fortunes by the Romans, at the time of Paul's conversion (A. D. 37) under the temporary rule of Aretas, king of Arabia Petræa (2 Cor. xi. 32). It is a paradise of beauty and fertility in the midst of a vast desert. It lies 133 miles northeast of Jerusalem, at the base of the Anti-Lebanon mountains, and is well watered by the Barada (Abana) and El A'way (Pharpar ; 2 Kings v. 12). This second visit to Damascus must fall within the 'many days' (a period of indefinite length) mentioned Acts ix. 23, and was terminated by the attempt of the Jews on his life (ix. 24, 25 ; 2 Cor. xi. 32). A window is still shown in the wall of Damascus, as the traditional scene of Paul's escape.

Ver. 18. Then after three years I went up to Jerusalem to make the acquaintance of (or, to become acquainted with) **Cephas, and remained with him fifteen days.** This first visit of Paul to Jerusalem after his conversion is the same as the one mentioned in Acts ix. 25, and took place A. D. 40. The 'three years' must be reckoned from his conversion (A. D. 37). It was quite natural that he should wish to make the personal acquaintance ('to see' in the English version is not strong enough) of Peter, the leader of the Twelve. The fact implies the high position of Peter, but no superior authority. Paul's object is to show that he was independent of human instruction and direction, and fully equal to the older Apostles. In ch. ii. 11, he relates that he even publicly reproved Peter at Antioch, which would have been an act of flagrant insubordination, had Peter been his superior in rank and authority. 'Cephas' is the reading of the best MSS. throughout this Epistle and the Epistle to the Corinthians, except Gal. ii. 7, 8, instead of 'Peter,' which arose from an explanatory gloss. This Syro-Chaldaic name was given to Simon by Christ (John i. 43), and was adhered to by the Judaizers. It was, perhaps, in silent opposition to them that Peter in his Epistles used the Greek form. — 'Fifteen days,' or, as we would say 'a fortnight,' — too short a time to become a disciple of Peter, as much of it was occupied by public disputations with the Hellenists. The reason of his short stay at Jerusalem was the persecution of the Greek Jews (Acts ix. 28, 29), and the express command of the Lord to go to the Gentiles (xxii. 17-21).

Ver. 19. But I saw no other of the Apostles but only James. The other Apostles were probably absent on a mission to the scattered churches of the provinces (comp. Acts ix. 31). The James here spoken of is not James the elder, the son of Zebedee and Salome, and brother of St. John, who was still living at that time (he was beheaded in 44 as the first martyr among the Apostles, Acts xii. 2), but the same who, after the departure of Peter from Palestine (xii. 17), presided over the congregation of Jerusalem (xv. 13 ; xxii. 18), and is frequently called 'brother of the Lord,' as here, or simply James (so in the Acts and Gal. ii.), or by the fathers 'Bishop of Jerusalem,' also 'James the Just.' Josephus, the Jewish historian, mentions him under the name of 'James the brother of Jesus, the so-called Christ,' and reports his martyrdom A. D. 62 (*Antiq.* xx. 9, 1). According to Hegesippus he died later, about A. D. 69. The exceptive words 'but only,' (or, 'if not,' 'save,' 'unless it be') do not necessarily imply that this James was one of the twelve Apostles, and identical with James the younger (who is called 'James the son of Alphæus') ; but it intimates rather, in connection with what precedes, and with his characteristic title here given, that he was, like Barnabas (Acts xiv. 14 ; comp. ix. 27), an Apostle only in the *wider* sense, who, owing to his character, position, and relationship to the Lord, enjoyed apostolical authority. The sense then is : 'the only other man of prominence and authority I saw was James.'[1]

The brother of the Lord. To distinguish him from the two Apostles of that name. 'Brother' is not cousin (for which Paul has the proper Greek term, Col. iv. 10), but either a uterine brother, *i. e.*, a younger son of Joseph and Mary (which is the most natural view ; comp. the words '*till*' and '*first* born' in Matt. i. 25, and Luke ii. 7) ; or a son of Joseph from a previous marriage, and hence a step-son of Mary and a step-brother of Jesus. Comp. on the brothers of the Lord (James, Joses, Simon, and Judas), Matt. i. 25 ; xii. 46 ; xiii. 55 ; Mark vi. 3 ; John ii. 12 ; vii. 3–10 ; Acts i. 14. The cousin-theory of the Roman church (dating from Jerome and Augustine at the close of the fourth century) is exegetically untenable, and was suggested chiefly by a doctrinal and ascetic bias in favor of the perpetual virginity of Mary and Joseph. The following reasons are conclusive against it and in favor of a closer relationship : (1.) the natural meaning of the term 'brother,' of which there is no exception in the New Testament, and scarcely in the Old ; (2.) the fact that these brothers and sisters appear in the Gospels constantly in close connection with the holy family ; (3.) they are represented as unbelieving before the resurrection (John vii. 5), which excludes them from the Twelve ; (4.) they are always distinguished from the Twelve (John ii. 17 ; vii. 3–10 ; Acts i. 14 ; 1 Cor. ix. 5). The old Greek fathers also (Origen, Eusebius, Epiphanius, etc.), clearly distinguish James the brother of the Lord from the two Apostles of that name.

---

[1] The question depends philologically upon the connection of the Greek particle εἰ μή. If connected with the whole sentence ('I saw no other Apostle save James'), it includes James among the Apostles ; if connected only with 'I saw' ('but *I saw* James'), it excludes him. The latter is the force of the particle in Gal. ii. 16 ; Matt. xii. 4 ; Luke iv 26, 27 ; Rev. xxi. 27. (See Wieseler's *Com.*)

Ver. 20. This solemn asseveration refers to the statement vers. 18 and 19. Judaizing opponents had probably spread the report in Galatia that Paul spent a much longer time in Jerusalem, and was instructed by the Jewish Apostles, especially by Peter, consequently dependent on them.

Ver. 21. Comp. Acts ix. 30. — **Syria**, the province of which Antioch was the capital. — **Cilicia**, the province adjoining Syria. Paul was a native of Tarsus, its capital, and a famous seat of learning. The object of his journey was no doubt to preach the gospel, as appears from Acts xv. 23, where churches are mentioned in those regions. In Tarsus, Barnabas met him somewhat later, and took him to Antioch, where they remained a whole year, and then they went together to Jerusalem (A. D. 44) on a benevolent mission (Acts xi. 25-30).

Ver. 22. **And was still unknown by face**, by sight, personally. — **Judæa** is here the district without the capital, as Italy is often distinguished from Rome (Heb. xiii. 24). The congregation of Jerusalem must be excepted; for there Paul was known from his visit mentioned in ver. 18, and from his former life when he studied at the feet of Gamaliel and persecuted the Christians. Comp. again Acts ix. 26-30.

Ver. 23. **They were hearing** (kept hearing) expresses the idea of duration better than 'heard.' — **The faith** is used here in the passive or objective sense = the gospel, the Christian religion (not a formulated statement of dogmas, but rather a living system of divine truth) ; comp. Gal. vi. 10 ; Acts vi. 7 ; Jude ver. 3. In most cases, however, especially in the Gospels, the Greek word has the active or subjective meaning, 'trust,' 'confidence' in God or Christ, and is one of the cardinal Christian virtues ; hence Christians are called 'believers.' If used of God, it means his faithfulness, trustworthiness, immutability of purpose (Rom. iii. 3).

Ver. 24. **In me**, in my case, or example, not on my account. The Christian hero-worship gives all the glory to God. Chrysostom: 'He does not say, they marvelled at me, they were struck with admiration of me, but he attributes all to grace. They glorified God, he says, in me.' This truly Christian conduct of the Jewish converts in Palestine contrasts favorably with the envy and calumny of the Judaizers in Galatia.

Excursus on the Conversion of St. Paul.

CHAPTER I. 13-17.

Here we have from Paul's own pen a brief account of his conversion, which coincided with his call to the apostleship. It is more fully related three times in the Acts, once by Luke (chap. ix.), and twice by Paul himself, before his countrymen at Jerusalem (chap. xxii.), and before King Agrippa (chap. xxvi.). He alludes to it repeatedly in his Epistles ; he saw the Lord Jesus Christ (1 Cor. ix. 1), who appeared to him on the way to Damascus as really and visibly as he had previously appeared to the older Apostles (1 Cor. xv. 8). We make a few reflections on this great event : —

1. The conversion of Paul was a miracle of divine grace, resting on the greater miracle of the resurrection of Christ. All attempts to explain it from external causes such as thunder and lightning, or out of a previous state of his mind, have failed. The most learned of modern skeptics (Dr. Baur) confessed at the end of his life (1860), that 'no psychological nor dialectical analysis' can explain this extraordinary transformation of Paul 'from the most vehement adversary into the most resolute herald of Christianity,' and he felt constrained to call it 'a miracle,' notwithstanding his philosophical aversion to miracles.

2. It was sudden and radical. Paul compares it to the creative act of God which called the natural light out of the darkness of chaos (2 Cor. iv. 6). He was in a state of active and fanatical hostility to Christ, bent upon the destruction of Christianity, and at once became a most determined and devoted champion of the cross he had hated and despised, and the most successful promoter of the religion he had hoped to exterminate from the face of the earth. The connecting link between the Jewish Saul and the Christian Paul was the honesty of purpose and the energy of will. Resolute and energetic characters are apt to change suddenly and radically, and to embrace the new cause with all the ardor of their soul. Upon proud, heroic natures the Spirit of God comes, not in the still, gentle breeze, but in the earthquake, the fire, and the storm. Augustine, Luther, Calvin, and Knox may be quoted as illustrations, although they fall far behind the great Apostle of the Gentiles.

3. It was as sincere as any conversion that ever took place. It cannot be explained from any selfish motive of gain or ambition. Paul was neither an impostor nor an enthusiast. He had nothing to win and everything to lose in a worldly point of view. He left a commanding position as a leader of the Jewish nation, to join a poor, weak, despised sect, which at first distrusted him ; he sacrificed honor, influence, and power for a life of toil, self-denial, and persecution. He suffered the loss of all things and 'counted them but dung that he might win Christ' (Phil. iii. 8, 9) ; and in Him he found the richest compensation for all his sacrifices.

4. It was lasting and most effective for all future ages. Paul labored more in word and deed than any other Apostle. He was a true moral conqueror of the world. His life and work after his conversion is, next to the life of his and our Lord and Master, the sublimest spectacle in the history of religion. It was one unbroken act of self-consecration to the glory of Christ and the good of mankind, and sealed at last with a joyful and triumphant martyrdom.

5. It is an unanswerable argument for the truth of Christianity. It is a regenerative, converting, ennobling, and sanctifying agency wherever Paul's name is known, his history read, and his Epistles studied in the fear and love of God. It has led to many conversions besides that of Lord Lyttleton, who wrote a special book on the subject. No other religion can produce such characters as Paul. A life so pure, so noble, so devoted, so fruitful in good works, is a perpetual benediction to the church and the world.

2

CHAPTER II.

I. Conference of Paul with the Elder Apostles at Jerusalem, vers. 1-10. II. Collision of Paul with Peter at Antioch, vers. 11-21.

Conference of Paul with the Jewish Apostles at Jerusalem.

CHAPTER II. 1-10.

Continuation of the personal defence. Fourteen years after his conversion, Paul had an interview with the Apostles of the circumcision at Jerusalem concerning his mode of preaching the gospel, and was recognized by them as an independent, divinely appointed Apostle of the Gentiles. With this section should be compared the account of the Apostolic Council in Acts xv.

Which journey to Jerusalem does Paul here refer to? This is the preliminary question to be settled in the interpretation of this difficult section. The Acts mention five such journeys after his conversion, namely: (1.) ix. 23 (comp. Gal. i. 18), the journey of the year 40, three years after his conversion. (2.) xi. 30; xii. 25 the journey during the famine in 44. (3.) xv. 2, the journey to the Apostolic Council, A. D. 50 or 51. (4.) xviii. 22, the journey in 54. (5.) xxi.'15 (comp. Rom. xv. 25 ff.), the last visit, on which he was made a prisoner and sent to Cæsarea, A. D. 58.

Of these journeys the first, of course, cannot be meant, on account of Gal. i. 18. The second is excluded by the chronological date in ii. 1. For as it took place during the famine of Palestine and in the year in which Herod died, A. D. 44, it would put the conversion of Paul back to the year 30, which is much too early. Some propose to read *four* instead of *fourteen*, but without any critical authority. There is no good reason why Paul should have mentioned this second journey, since it was undertaken simply for the transmission of a collection of the Christians at Antioch for the relief of the brethren in Judæa, and not for the purpose of conferring with the Apostles on matters of dispute. In all probability he saw none of them on that occasion, since in that year a persecution raged in which James the elder suffered martyrdom, and Peter was imprisoned. The fifth journey cannot be meant, as it took place after the composition of the Epistle to the Galatians and after the dispersion of the Apostles. Nor can we think of the fourth, which was very short and transient (Acts xviii. 21, 22), leaving no time for such important transactions as are here alluded to; nor was Barnabas with him on that occasion, having separated from Paul some time before (Acts xv. 39).

We must therefore identify our journey with the third one, mentioned in the 15th chapter of Acts. For this took place A. D. 50 or 51, *i. e.*, fourteen years after his conversion (37), and was occasioned by the controversy on the authority of the law of Moses and the relation of the Gentile converts to the Christian Church (Acts xv. 2). This visit Paul could not pass over, as it was of the greatest moment to his argument. The two accounts perfectly agree in all the essential circumstances. The conference took place between Jerusalem and Antioch; the persons are the same, Cephas and James representing the Jewish Christians in Jerusalem, Paul and Barnabas delegated from Antioch in behalf of the Gentile Christians; the Judaizing agitators are the same; the controversy is the same, namely, the circumcision; the result is the same, namely, the triumph of the principle of faith in the saving grace of Christ, and the recognition of the Apostolic authority of Paul and Barnabas for the mission among the Gentiles. But the account of the Acts is fuller; that of the Galatians only brings out the chief points. Luke, in keeping with the documentary character of the Acts, gives us the *public* transactions of the Council at Jerusalem; Paul, taking a knowledge of these for granted, shortly alludes to his *private* conference and agreement with the Apostles (see note to verse 2). Both together give us a complete history of that remarkable convention. It was the first synod in Christendom for the settlement of the first doctrinal and practical controversy which agitated the church and threatened to divide it; but the wisdom of the Apostles prevented the split.

1 THEN fourteen years after [1] [a] I went up again to Jerusalem [a] Acts xv. 2.
2 with Barnabas, and took Titus with *me* also.[2] And I went up by revelation, [b] and communicated unto them that [3] gospel [b] Acts xv. 12.

[1] after an interval, *or,* after the lapse of fourteen years
[2] having taken with me Titus also
[3] laid before them (*or,* referred to them) the

which I preach among the Gentiles, but privately to them which *c* Phil. ii. 16;
1 Thess. iii.
were of reputation,[4] lest by any means *e* I should run, or had   5; 1 Cor. ix.
24.
3 run, in vain.[5]   But neither[6] Titus, who was with me, being a *d* Acts xv. 1,
24; 2 Cor.
4 Greek, was compelled to be circumcised : And that[7] because of *e* Chap. iii. 25;
d false brethren unawares brought in,[8] who came in[9] privily to   chap. v. 1,
13.
spy out our *e* liberty which we have in Christ Jesus, *f* that they *f* 2 Cor. xi. 20;
chap. iv. 3,
5 might bring us into bondage : To whom we gave place by sub-   9, 24, 25;
ver. 1.
jection, no, not for an hour;[10] that *g* the truth of the gospel *g* Ver. 14;
chap. iii. 1;
6 might continue with you.   But of those *h* who seemed to be   chap. iv. 16.
h chap. vi. 3.
somewhat[11] (whatsoever they were,[12] it maketh no matter to *i* Rom. ii. 11.
k 2 Cor. xii.
me : *i* God accepteth no[13] man's person), for they who seemed   11.
l Acts xiii. 46;
7 *to be somewhat* *k* in conference added nothing to me :[14] But   Rom. i. 5;
Rom. xi. 13;
contrariwise,[15] *l* when they saw that the gospel of the uncir-   1 Tim. ii. 7;
2 Tim. i. 11.
cumcision *m* was committed unto me,[16] as *the gospel* of the cir- *m* 1 Thess. ii.
4.
8 cumcision *was* unto Peter;[17] (For he that wrought effectually *n* Acts ix. 15;
xiii. 2; xxii.
in Peter to[18] the apostleship of the circumcision, *n* the same   21; xxvi. 17,
18; 1 Cor.
9 was *o* mighty in me toward[19] the Gentiles ;) And when[20] James,   xv. 10;
chap. i. 16;
Cephas, and John, who seemed to be *p* pillars,[21] perceived[22]   Col. i. 29.
o Chap. iii. 5.
q the grace that was given unto me, they[23] gave to me and *p* Matt. xvi.
18; Eph. ii
Barnabas the right hands of fellowship, that we *should go*[24]   20; Rev.
xxi. 14.
10 unto the heathen,[25] and they unto the circumcision ; only *they* *q* Rom. i. 5;
xii. 3. 6;
would[26] that we should remember the poor ; *r* the same which   xv. 15; 1
Cor. xv. 10;
I also was forward to do.[27]   Eph. iii. 8.
r Acts xi. 30;
xxiv. 17;
[4] before those of (chief) reputation   Rom. xv.
25; 1 Cor.
[5] lest perchance I might be running, or had run to no purpose   xvi. 1; 2
Cor. viii., ix.
[6] Yet not even   [7] or, but *it was*
[8] on account of the false brethren stealthily (insidiously) brought in, *or,*
   foisted in   [9] *lit.* came in besides, *or,* crept in
[10] we did not yield even for an hour by submission (*or,* in the way of submission)
[11] from those reputed to be something (those in authority)
[12] *or,* what they once were   [13] not
[14] for to me those of (chief) reputation added nothing (*or,* gave me no new
   instruction)   [15] on the contrary   [16] that I am intrusted with
[17] even as Peter *with that* of the uncircumcision
[18] who gave strength to Peter for   [19] gave strength to me also for
[20] *omit* when   [21] who are reputed to be pillars
[22] perceiving   [23] *omit* they
[24] *others supply* that we should preach the gospel to, *or,* should be apostles to
[25] Gentiles   [26] *omit* they would
[27] the very thing which I also was zealous to do

Ver. 1. **Then after an interval of fourteen years
I went up again to Jerusalem.** The fourteen years
of independent apostolic labor are to be reckoned
not from the journey last mentioned (i. 18), but
from Paul's conversion, this being the great turning point in his life (i. 15). As this probably took
place A. D. 37, we would have the year 50 or 51
for the Apostolic Council here referred to.   This

date is confirmed by other chronological hints and
combinations.   The second journey to Jerusalem,
on a purely benevolent mission during the famine
of 44, at a season of persecution when probably
all the Apostles were absent and only " the Elders" are mentioned (Acts xi. 30; xii. 25), is
omitted as irrelevant to the point here at issue.
After my conversion, he means to say, I had the

following opportunities of conferring with the Apostles: (1.) three years afterwards I went to Jerusalem, and saw Peter, but only for a fortnight; (2.) after a lapse of fourteen years I went to Jerusalem again and had a special conference with the chief Apostles. But in neither case was I instructed or commissioned by them; on the contrary, they recognized me as an independent, divinely appointed Apostle of the Gentiles.

Lightfoot also identifies this visit with that to the Apostolic Council, which he puts into the year 51, but dates the fourteen years from the first visit (i. 18), and throws the first visit back to A. D. 38, and the conversion to A. D. 36, adopting the Jewish mode of reckoning.

With Barnabas, having taken with me Titus also. Barnabas, next to Paul the chief leader of the Gentile mission, is mentioned by Luke (Acts xv. 2) as his fellow-delegate from Antioch. Titus is nowhere mentioned in the Acts, but included in the 'certain others,' who accompanied them. Being an uncircumcised convert and a living testimony of the efficient labors of Paul among the Gentiles, Titus was peculiarly suited for the object of this journey. He was also (as Lightfoot suggests) much in Paul's mind, if not in his company, at the time he wrote this Epistle (comp. 2 Cor. ii. 13; vii. 6, 13-15; viii. 16, 23; xii. 18).

Ver. 2. **By revelation.** In consequence of a divine monition such as he often experienced (comp. Acts xvi. 6, 7; xix. 21; xx. 22, 23; xxii. 17; xxvii. 23; 2 Cor. xii. 1). This was the inward, personal motive. Luke in Acts xv. 2 omits this, but mentions the external, or public occasion, namely, the appointment by the church of Antioch, which sent him and Barnabas as delegates to represent the interests of Gentile Christianity. This appointment may have been either prompted or confirmed by the inner revelation. So Peter, according to Acts x., was induced both by a vision and by the messengers of Cornelius, to go to Cæsarea. — **And communicated to them,** or **laid before them,** i. e., the Christians at Jerusalem (ver. 1), the whole congregation. This implies a public transaction in open council, which is described in the Acts. Paul confines himself to an account of the private and personal agreement with the leading Apostles, because the decision and pastoral letter of the council (Acts xv. 22 ff.) had already been communicated by him to his churches (xvi. 4). The decree was a compromise intended for a special emergency, and not for universal and permanent use. But it was no doubt interpreted by the Judaizing teachers in a sense contrary to the meaning of the chief Apostles, and hence the importance of referring to their personal understanding with Paul. — **Privately,** or apart, in private conference, as distinct from the discussion in open council. Such private conferences are always held in connection with public assemblies, for the purpose of preparing and maturing business for final action. Bengel: 'All were not capable of comprehending it.' — **Those of chief reputation,** the leading men who enjoyed the greatest authority among the Jewish Christians, the 'pillar' Apostles, namely James, Peter, and John (ver. 9). Similar is the expression, 'the very chiefest Apostles' (2 Cor. xi. 5; xii. 11). 'The men of chief reputation' is a term of honor, but as repeated in vers. 6 and 9 in connection with 'something,' and 'pillars,' it seems to imply a slight tint of irony. The blame is, of course, not intended for the

Apostles themselves, whose testimony in his favor it is his purpose here to relate, and whom he always treated with fraternal esteem and love, but for the Judaizers who unduly exalted them above Paul. He feels himself equal to them before men, and yet in his deep humility before God he calls himself the least of the Apostles and unworthy of the high name, because he persecuted the church of God (1 Cor. xv. 9). See Excursus. — **Lest perchance,** etc., lest my apostolic labors past and present should be fruitless, not in themselves nor in the judgment of Paul, but in the judgment of the Jewish Christians. The non-recognition of the Gentile churches by the mother church of Jerusalem would have interfered also with the progress of his mission and unsettled many of his weaker converts, as the example of the Galatians shows. The expression 'run' is taken from the image of a race, to which the Christian life is frequently compared (Phil. ii. 16; 2 Tim. iv. 7; 1 Cor. vii. 24 f.; Gal. v. 7; Heb. xii. 1). Bengel: 'I should run with the swift victory of the gospel.'

Ver. 3. **Yet not even Titus .... being a Greek,** or although he was a Greek, that is, a heathen. Far from declaring my labors fruitless and disapproving my gospel, the Jewish Apostles did not force even Titus, my companion and co-laborer, much less the body of the Gentile converts, to submit to circumcision, although the Judaizing party peremptorily demanded it as a condition of justification (as appears from vers. 4 and 5, and Acts xv. 5).

Ver. 4. **And that** (happened, or, was done) **on account of the false brethren.** The words 'and that' (δέ = nempe) are explanatory, and assign the reason why Titus was not compelled by the chief Apostles to be circumcised. It explains and qualifies the general assertion (ver. 3), and intimates that under other circumstances, if no principles had been involved, and if the false brethren had not made it a party issue, the Jewish Apostles might have demanded or at least recommended circumcision, as an act of prudence, or for peace sake. Paul would have respected the scruples of *weak* brethren (comp. Rom. xiv. and xv.); while he was inflexible in resisting the demands of *false* brethren. He himself, after the apostolic council, circumcised Timothy (Acts xvi. 3) without any inconsistency (comp. 1 Cor. vii. 18). For he did this from his own impulse, and for the purpose of making Timothy more useful, without compromising the principle of justification by faith. It must be remembered, also, that Timothy was a Jew from his mother's side, and that therefore the Jews had a certain right to claim him, while Titus was a pure Gentile by birth.

Others take ver. 4 as an independent, though grammatically irregular sentence, and supplement it in this way: 'But (δέ in the adversative sense) on account of the false brethren (i. e., to appease the Judaizers) *the leading Apostles* RECOMMENDED *the circumcision of Titus as a charitable concession to their prejudices* — to whom, however (i. e., the false brethren), we (*Paul and Barnabas*) did not yield for a single hour.' This would imply a slight censure of the weakness of the other Apostles. Paul was, we must suppose in this case, distracted between the duty of frankness and the duty of reserve; he wished to maintain his independence without compromising his colleagues. Hence the broken and obscure character of the sentence.

Foisted in, brought in by unfair means, like traitors and spies. These Judaizers were formerly Pharisees (Acts xv. 5), and were so still in spirit, although they professed Christianity by the mouth and were baptized. From these *false* brethren who were intolerant Judaizers of the malignant type and bitter haters of freedom, we should carefully distinguish the *weak* brethren whom Paul treats with great indulgence (Rom. xiv. 1 ; xv. 1-3).—**To spy out,** or to act as spies on our freedom from the bondage of the law, and to find out how far we observed the Mosaic ordinances or violated them.—**In Christ Jesus,** in living union with him who is the end and fulfilment of the law (Rom. x. 4). This is the positive side of freedom. Out of Christ there is no true freedom, but slavery of sin (comp. v. 1-12 ; John viii. 32-36).

Ver. 5. These false brethren, it must be remembered, required circumcision and the observance of the whole ceremonial law not only from the Jewish, but also from the Gentile Christians, and that not only as an old venerable custom, but as a necessary condition to salvation. Paul and his companions could, therefore, not yield to them for a moment **by the submission** (required by the false brethren) to the law of circumcision, so as to circumcise Titus according to their demand. He could here not become a Jew to the Jews in order to gain them (1 Cor. ix. 20-22), as in such cases where the truth was not jeopardized, and where subjection was simply a matter of charity and expediency. Submission in the case of Titus would have been treason to the truth that Christ is the only and sufficient source of salvation ; it would have been a sacrifice of the sacred rights and liberty of the Gentile Christians. Bengel takes 'submission' as a limitation : ' We would willingly have yielded for *love.*'

Ver. 6. **From those reputed to be something ;** lit., 'those who have the estimation of being something,' that is, something great, or 'those who are held in chief reputation,' ' who are looked up to as authorities,' the 'pillar'-apostles, ver. 9, or as Paul expresses it in 2 Cor. xi. 5 and xii. 11, 'the very chiefest apostles.' It appears from ver. 9 that he means the older Apostles, James, Peter, and John, who were justly regarded as the pillars of the Church. The expression may be depreciatory (comp. Gal. vi. 3), according to the context. He does not, as already remarked, depreciate his colleagues, but disapproves the extravagant overestimate put upon them by the Judaizers in behalf of their own narrow and exclusive system and in opposition to Paul. His high sense of independence, far from being identical with pride, rested in his humility and was but the complement to his feeling of absolute dependence on God.—' **What they once** (formerly) **were,**' refers to their advantages in the personal intercourse with Christ, on which the Judaizers laid great stress, and on which they based the superiority of the Twelve. Paul made no account of the knowledge of Christ ' after the flesh ' (2 Cor. v. 16), which was of no benefit to the Jews without faith.—**God accepteth not man's person,** or God is no regarder of person. A Hebraizing expression for impartiality. To regard a man's person, his face, wealth, rank, and external condition, as distinct from his intrinsic merits, is partiality, and this God never exercises (comp. Acts x. 34; Rom. ii. 11 ; Eph. vi. 9; Col. iii. 25).—**For to me those,** I say,—reassumption of the unfinished sentence in another form, instead of : ' From those of chief reputation—I received no new instruction.'—**Added** (or **communicated, imparted**) **nothing,** *i. e.,* by way of supplementing or correcting my exposition of the Gospel (ver. 2), but on the contrary they were satisfied with it and with my mode of converting the Gentiles. (Others explain : laid no *additional burden* on me, namely, the ceremonial law ; but they laid no burden on him at all.)

Ver. 7. **When they saw,** from the communications of Paul (ver. 2) and the abundant results of his missionary labors among the Gentiles (Acts xv. 12).—**That I am** (not **was**) **intrusted.** I have been and am still intrusted. The Greek perfect implies that the commission and trust is still in active force.—**With the gospel of uncircumcision,** *i. e.,* with the evangelization of the Gentiles. The gospel is the same, but the sphere of labor is different. Paul was directed to the field of heathen missions at his conversion (which coincided with his call and apostleship), Acts ix. 15, and more clearly by a special revelation in the temple of Jerusalem, xxii. 17-21. Yet the division of labor was not absolute and exclusive. Paul generally commenced to preach in the synagogue because it furnished the most convenient locality and the natural, historical connection for the announcement of the gospel, and because it was resorted to by the numerous proselytes who formed the bridge to heathen missions (comp. Acts xiii. 5, 46; xiv. 1 ; xviii. 6 ; Rom. i. 16 ; ix. 1, 3). On the other hand, Peter, though he was then, and continued to be, the head of the Jewish Christian branch of the Apostolic Church, opened the door for the conversion of the Gentiles by the baptism of Cornelius (Acts x. ; xi. ; xv. 7), and his Epistles show that in his later years he did not confine himself to the circumcision, for the congregations to which they are addressed were of a mixed character and partly founded by Paul.

Ver. 8 is a parenthetic explanation of ver. 7.—**Gave strength to** (or **worked for**), *i. e.,* enabled them successfully to discharge the duties of the Apostolic office, by conferring upon them the necessary spiritual gifts and qualifications and accompanying their preaching with signs and miracles (comp. Rom. xv. 18, 19 ; 2 Cor. xii. 12).—**For the Gentiles**—for the apostleship of the Gentiles.

Ver. 9. **Perceiving** (or **knowing**) indicates the conviction arrived at in consequence of the successful labors of Paul, as the divine attestation of his apostleship.—**The grace** implies here the call, the spiritual outfit and the success, all of which Paul regards as a free gift of God in Christ, as he says, 1 Cor. xv. 10 : ' By the grace of God I am what I am ; and his grace which was bestowed upon me was not in vain ; but I labored more abundantly than they all ; yet not I, but the grace of God which was with me.'—**James** stands here first according to the best manuscripts. It is the brother of the Lord, mentioned i. 19. Although not one of the Twelve, he enjoyed Apostolic authority. (There is no good reason for understanding here, with Dr. Wieseler, the younger Apostle of that name, James the son of Alphæus, who held no very prominent rank. The older James, the son of Zebedee, suffered martyrdom in 44, six years before the Council of Jerusalem.) In the Jewish Church at large Peter occupied the most prominent rank, and is therefore named in vers. 7 and 8 ; but in Jerusalem, of which Paul speaks here, James stood at the head of the congregation (comp. Acts xii. 17; xv. 13; xxi. 18), and he probably presided also over the Apostolical Council, or at all events exerted the controlling influence there and led to the final decision, Acts xv. 13 ff. — **Pillars,** *i. e.*, leading men, chief champions of the church, which is often represented as a temple, 1 Cor. v. 16; Eph. ii. 21; 1 Tim. iii. 15; Rev. iii. 12. But the expression is used in the same sense in all languages without metaphor, and especially among the Jews of the great teachers of the law. Paul does not deny his colleagues to be the leading Apostles of the Jews; they were so still in fact, as he was the pillar of the Gentile Church; but the Judaizers used the expression no doubt in an envious party sense and with the view to depreciate Paul (comp. ver. 6 note). — **The right hands of fellowship.** A pledge of brotherhood and fidelity. This fact, based as it was, on sincere esteem and love, refutes the conclusion of some modern critics that there was a serious discord between Paul and the older Apostles. They differed widely, no doubt, in talent, temperament, and field of labor, but they agreed in spirit and principle; they were servants to the same Lord and organs of the same grace, and as they sought not their own glory, there was no room for envy and jealousy. — **That we should** (*go,* or, *be Apostles,* or, *preach the gospel*) **to the Gentiles and they to the circumcision,** *i. e.*, the Jews. Division of the field of labor, with one reservation, mentioned in ver. 10, and faithfully kept.

Ver. 10. **Remember the poor** of the Jewish Christians in Palestine, who suffered much from famine and persecution (comp. Acts. xi. 29). Charity should thus not only afford temporal relief to the needy, but be a moral bond of union also between the Jewish and the Gentile Christians and furnish a proof of the gratitude of the latter for the unspeakable gift of the gospel which they received from the former. Such a collection is mentioned Acts xi. 29 f., and was forwarded by the congregation of Antioch to the brethren in Judæa through the hands of Paul and Barnabas during the famine of 44. On his third great missionary tour between 54 and 57, Paul raised large contributions in his congregations for this purpose, and took then himself to Jerusalem on his fifth and last visit (1 Cor. xvi. 1; 2 Cor. viii. and ix.; Rom. xv. 25; Acts xxiv. 17). — **The very thing which I was zealous** (diligently endeavored) **to do,** then and always. He needed no prompting to this duty and privilege. It was his habit, and hence the Judaizers had no ground whatever to charge him with a breach of contract on that score. The exercise of Christian liberality and benevolence for the poor, for missions and all the general operations of the Church, is as much a duty and ought to be as steady a habit, as prayer, or any other exercise of piety. What Paul did in the Apostolic age, has been done by the Church ever since. The West receives the gospel from the East and must show its gratitude by helping the East. If pure Christianity is to be revived in Bible Lands it must be done by the faith and the money of the Churches of Europe and America.

Excursus on the Relation of Paul to the Jewish Apostles.

CHAPTER II. 1-10.

Compare here my *History of the Apostolic Church* (1853), pp. 245-260 and pp. 282 ff., 616 ff., and an able Excursus of Dr. Lightfoot on ' St Paul and the Three,' in his *Com. on Galat.*, p. 283 ff. (second ed. 1866).

The Epistle to the Galatians and the entire history of the Apostolic Church cannot be understood without keeping constantly in view the fact that the Apostolic Church embraced two distinct, and yet essentially harmonious sections of *Jewish* and *Gentile Christians,* which ultimately grew together into one community. The distinction disappeared after the destruction of Jerusalem, when the last link between the old and the new religion was broken. Before that event there was more or less friction arising from educational prejudices and congenial surroundings. In the second chapter of the Galatians and the fifteenth chapter of the Acts the friction is distinctly brought out, and, at the same time, the underlying Apostolic harmony. In the second century the antagonism without the harmony reappeared in the distorted and heretical forms of the Judaizing Ebionitism and the antinomian Gnosticism.

The Jewish Christianity clung closely to the Mosaic traditions and usages and hoped for a conversion of the Jewish nation until that hope was annihilated by the terrible judgment of the destruction of the temple, and the Jewish theocracy. The Gentile Christianity was free from those traditions and established on a liberal and independent basis. The older Apostles, especially James, Peter, and John (in his earlier period) represented the church of the circumcision (ver. 9); James the brother of the Lord and head of the mother church at Jerusalem, being the most strict and conservative, Peter the most authoritative, John the most liberal and holding himself in mysterious reserve for his later comprehensive position. Paul and Barnabas represented the Apostolate of the Gentiles, and the independent, progressive-type of Christianity.

Once, and as far as we know, once only these great leaders of Apostolic Christianity came together for public and private conference, at Jerusalem, to decide the great and vital question whether Christianity should be forever confined to the narrow limits of Jewish traditions with circumcision as the necessary term of membership, or whether it should break through these boundaries and become as universal as the human race on the sole basis of a living faith in Christ as the all-sufficient Saviour of men. Of this critical turning point we have but two accounts, one from the chief actor on the part of a free gospel for the Gentiles, in the second chapter of this Epistle, and one from his pupil and companion, Luke, in the fifteenth chapter of the Acts. Neither James, Peter, or John make any direct allusion to these memorable transactions. The two accounts are not contradictory, but supplementary. Both represent the conference as a sharp controversy, ending in a peaceful understanding which saved the unity of the Church. The great principle for which Paul contended triumphed, that faith in Christ alone, without circumcision, is necessary to salvation, and consequently that circumcision should not be imposed upon the Gentile converts. Without this principle Christianity could never have conquered the world. On the other hand a temporary concession was made to the Jewish party, namely that the Gentiles should "abstain from meats offered to idols, and from blood, and from things strangled, and from fornication," that is from practices which were peculiarly offensive to the conscience of the Jews. Paul was fully recognized by the Jewish Apostles as the Apostle of the Gentiles and received from them the right hand of fellowship and brotherhood on the sole condition that he should remember the poor brethren in Judæa by the exercise of practical charity, which he had done before and which he did afterwards with all his heart.

Nevertheless the old controversy continued, not, indeed, among the Apostles (excepting the dispute between Peter and Paul, at Antioch, which referred only to conduct, not to doctrine), but among the unconverted Pharisaical Judaizers and Paul; and the whole career of the great Apostle of the Gentiles was a continual struggle against those pseudo-apostles who could never forget that he had been a fanatical persecutor, and, who looked upon him as a dangerous radical. To this life-long conflict we owe his greatest Epistles, especially the Galatians and the Romans, with their vigorous defence of Christian liberty and their profound expositions of the doctrines of sin and grace. Thus error has been providentially overruled for the exposition and vindication of truth. (See the next Excursus on Paul and Peter.)

The Collision of Paul with Peter at Antioch.

CHAPTER II. 11-21.

Paul continues to prove his independent Apostolic dignity, and shows that he asserted it even in open opposition to Peter at Antioch before the mother congregation of Gentile Christianity, when the latter acted inconsistently with his own view concerning our justification before God, and in a moment of weakness betrayed the cause of the Gentiles by yielding to the pressure of the Judaizing ritualists. Then Paul stood all alone as the champion of Christian liberty. In ver. 15 he passes from the personal and historical part to the doctrinal part, namely, the defence of his evangelical view of the way of salvation in opposition to the Judaizing legalism of the false teachers.

The Acts make no mention of this controversy with Peter, but they relate a dispute between Paul and Barnabas (xv. 36-40), which took place likewise at Antioch soon after the Apostolic conference, and although referring mainly to a personal matter concerning Mark, was in all probability connected with the other dispute, inasmuch as Barnabas suffered himself to be led into a similar inconsistency by the example of Peter (Gal. ii. 2, 13).

11 [a] BUT when Peter[1] was come[2] to Antioch, I withstood him [a] Acts xv. 35:
12 to the face, because he was to be blamed.[3] For before
   that certain came[4] from James, [b] he did eat[5] with the Gen- [b] Acts x. 28; xi. 3. Comp.
   tiles: but when they were come,[6] he withdrew and separated   Luke xv. 2.
13 himself, fearing them *which were* of the circumcision.[7] And
   the other Jews dissembled likewise with him; insomuch that
14 Barnabas also[8] was carried away with their dissimulation. But
   when I saw that they walked not uprightly[9] according to [c] the [c] Ver. 5.
   truth of the gospel, I said unto Peter[10] [d] before *them*[11] all, [e] If [d] 1 Tim. v. 20.
   thou, being a Jew, livest after the manner of Gentiles, and not [e] Ver. 12; Acts x. 28; xi. 3.

---

[1] Cephas (*according to the best authorities*)   [2] came
[3] he was condemned   [4] before the coming of certain *persons*
[5] he used to eat together with   [6] came
[7] those of the circumcision   [8] so that even Barnabas   [9] straight
[10] Cephas   [11] *omit them*

as do the Jews,[12] why compellest thou the Gentiles to live as do the Jews?[13]

15 *f* We *who are* Jews by nature, and not *g* sinners of the Gen-
16 tiles,[14] *h* Knowing[15] that a man is not justified by the works of the law,[16] but *i* by the faith of[17] Jesus Christ, even we have believed[18] in Jesus Christ, that we might be justified by the faith of[19] Christ, and not by the works of the law:[16] for *k* "by
17 the works of the law[16] shall no flesh be justified." But if, while we seek[20] to be justified by[21] Christ, we ourselves also are[22] *l* found *l* sinners, *is* therefore Christ the[23] minister of sin? God *m*
18 forbid.[24] For if I build again the things which I destroyed, I *n*
19 make[25] myself a transgressor. For I *m* through the[26] law *n* am *o*
20 dead to the law,[27] that I might *o* live unto God. I am[28] *p* crucified with Christ: nevertheless I live;[29] yet not I,[30] but Christ liveth in me: and the life which I now live[31] in the flesh *q* I *p* live by the faith of the son of God,[32] *r* who loved me, and gave
21 himself for me. I do not frustrate the grace of God: for *s* if righteousness *come* by the law, then Christ is dead in vain.[33]

f Acts xv. 10. 22.
g Ver. 17; Matt. ix. 11; Eph. ii. 3 11, 12.
h Acts xiii. 38 39; xv. 11.
i iii. 24; Rom i. 17; iii. 22 28; viii. 3.
k Ps. cxliii. 2, Rom. iii. 20; chap. iii. 11.
l Ver. 15; Eph. ii. 3, 11, 12.
m Rom. viii. 2.
n Rom. vi. 14; vii. 4, 6. Rom. vi. 11; 2 Cor. v. 15; 1 Thess. v. 10; Heb. ix. 14; 1 Peter iv. 2.
o Rom. vi. 6; chap. v. 24; chap. vi. 14. 2 Cor. v. 15; 1 Thess. v. 10; 1 Peter iv. 2.
r Chap. i. 4; Eph. v. 2; Tit. ii. 14.
s Chap. iii. 21; Heb. vii. 11; See Rom. xi. 6; chap. v. 4.

[12] livest as the Gentiles and not as the Jews
[13] how is it that thou constrainest the Gentiles to Judaize (*or*, to live as the Jews)
[14] We being Jews by nature, and not sinners from among the Gentiles
[15] yet knowing   [16] by works of law   [17] but only through faith in
[18] even we ourselves became believers   [19] by faith in   [20] sought
[21] in   [22] were   [23] a   [24] Let it never be (Far from it)
[25] if I build up again the very things which I pulled down, I prove
[26] *omit* the   [27] died unto law   [28] have been
[29] *omit* nevertheless I live   [30] and it is no longer I that live
[31] that which I now live (*or*, so far as I now live)
[32] in faith which is in the Son of God   [33] died without cause (gratuitously)

Ver. 11. The scene here related is of great importance for the history of Apostolic Christianity, but has often been misunderstood and distorted both in the interest of orthodoxy and heresy. It took place between the Apostolic conference (A. D. 50) and the second great missionary journey of Paul (A. D. 51). To the same period must be assigned the personal dispute between Paul and Barnabas on account of Mark, related in Acts xv. 30–40. Barnabas followed the bad example of Peter (ver. 13), and Mark would naturally sympathize with Barnabas, his cousin (Col. iv. 10), and with Peter, his spiritual father (1 Pet. v. 13). There was, therefore, a double reason for the temporary alienation of Paul and Barnabas. It appears that soon after the council at Jerusalem a misunderstanding arose as to the precise bearing of the decree of the council (Acts xv. 20, 29). That decree was both emancipating and restrictive; it emancipated the Gentile converts from circumcision as a test of church membership (on the observance of which the Pharisaical Judaizers, or 'false brethren' had vainly insisted), but it laid on them the restriction of observing the precepts traditionally traced to Noah (comp. Gen. ix. 4, 5) and required from 'proselytes of the gate,' namely, the abstinence from 'meats offered to idols, and from blood, and from things strangled, and from fornication' (including probably unlawful marriages within the forbidden degrees of kindred, Lev. xvii. 18). The decree was framed to meet a special temporary emergency and certain specific complaints of the Jewish converts against the Gentile brethren in regard to these detested practices. But the decree made no direct provision for the conduct of the Jewish Christians, who were supposed to know their duty from the law read every Sabbath in the synagogues (xv. 21). And it was on this point that the difference of a *strict* and a *liberal* construction seems to have arisen. The logic of the decree pointed to a full communion with the Gentile brethren, but the letter did not. It was a compromise, a step in the right direction, but it stopped half way. It left the Levitical law concerning clean and unclean meats untouched (Luke xi. 4 ff., comp. Acts x. 14).[1] The heretical

[1] Augustine distinguishes three periods in the ceremonial

Judaizers considered the whole ceremonial law as binding upon all; James and the conservative Jewish brethren as binding only upon Jews; Paul and Peter as abrogated by the death of Christ. The conservative party at Jerusalem, under the lead of James, understood the decree as not justifying any departure of the circumcised Christians from their traditional rites and habits, and continued to maintain a cautious reserve towards Gentile Christians and all uncircumcised or unclean persons (Luke xv. 2; Acts x. 28), without, however, demanding circumcision; while the more liberal Jewish Christians at Antioch, encouraged by the powerful example of Peter, who had been freed from narrow prejudices by his vision at Joppa, and eaten with the uncircumcised Cornelius at Cæsarea (Acts x. 27, 28; xi. 3), associated with their Gentile brethren in social intercourse, and disregarded in their common meals the distinction between clean and unclean animal food; they may possibly even have innocently partaken of meat offered to idols, which was freely sold at the shambles, or at all events they ran the risk of doing so. Paul considered this as a matter in itself indifferent and harmless, considering the vanity of idols, *provided* that no offence be given to weak brethren, in which case he himself would 'eat no flesh for evermore,' lest he make his 'brother to stumble' (1 Cor. viii. 7-13; x. 23-33; Rom. xiv. 1-4); while as to fornication of any kind he condemned it absolutely as defiling the body which is the temple of God (1 Cor. v. 1-13; vi. 18-20). This freedom as to eating with Gentiles threatened to break up a part of the Jerusalem compromise and alarmed the conservative Jews. Hence the remonstrance from Jerusalem which prevailed on the timid and impulsive Peter, and all the Jewish members of the congregation at Antioch, even Barnabas, but provoked the vigorous protest of Paul who stood alone in defence of Christian liberty and brotherhood on that trying occasion. This view of the matter seems to afford the best explanation of the conduct of both James and Peter, without justifying it; for Peter certainly denied his own better conviction that God is no respecter of persons (Acts x. 34), or that in Christ there is neither Greek nor Jew (as Paul expresses it, Col. iii. 24), and once more denied his Lord in the person of his Gentile disciples. The alienation, however, was only temporary, and did not result in a split of the church.

The residence of Peter at Antioch gave rise to the tradition that he founded the church there (A. D. 44, according to the *Chronicle* of Eusebius) before he transferred his see to Rome. The tradition also perpetuated the memory of the quarrel in dividing the church of Antioch into two parishes with two bishops, Evodius and Ignatius, the one instituted by Peter, the other by Paul.

Cephas is the Apostle Peter mentioned ver. 9, and not one of the seventy disciples, as Clement of Alexandria and other fathers (also the Jesuit Harduin) arbitrarily assumed in order to clear Peter of all blame. — **I withstood him to the face,** personally, not secretly or behind the back. It was a very bold act of Paul, requiring the highest order of moral courage. It seems inconsistent with the harmony of the Apostolic church and to reflect

too severely on Peter, the prince of the Apostles. Hence it has always been a stumbling block to those who believe, contrary to the explicit confessions of the Apostles themselves (1 John i. 8; James iii. 2; Phil. iii. 12), that their inspiration implied also their moral perfection, or that doctrinal infallibility is inseparable from practical impeccability. Several of the most eminent fathers, Origen, Jerome, and Chrysostom, tried to escape the difficulty by a misinterpretation of the words 'to the face,' as if they meant, 'according to appearance only' (*secundum speciem*), not in reality, and assumed that the dispute had been previously arranged by the Apostles for the purpose of convincing, not Peter, who was right all along, but the Jewish Christian members of the congregation, that the ceremonial law was now abolished. This most unnatural interpretation makes bad worse, by charging the hypocrisy upon both Paul and Peter, and turning the whole scene into a theatrical farce. St. Augustine, from a superior moral sense, protested against it, and Jerome himself tacitly abandoned it afterwards for the right view. The author of the Pseudo-Clementine Homilies (an Ebionite fiction of the second century, xvii. 19) understands the passage correctly, but makes it the ground of an attack on St. Paul (under the name of Simon Magus) by Peter, who says to him: 'Thou hast withstood me to my face.... If thou callest me condemned, thou accusest God who revealed Christ to me.' — **He was condemned,** self-condemned, self-convicted by his own conduct, not by the Gentile Christians of Antioch, for Paul would hardly have waited for the judgment of others in a matter of such importance. The inconsistency carried in it its own condemnation, as Paul proves (ver. 15-21). The translation 'he was blamed' is not strong enough, and the translation of the E. V. 'he was to be blamed,' or reprehensible, deserving of censure, is ungrammatical and lame.

Ver. 12. **Certain persons from James,** not simply members of his congregation at Jerusalem, but followers, and (as the word 'from' seems to indicate) delegates of James of Jerusalem (ver. 9), and invested with some authority, which they abused. We are not to understand by them 'false brethren' (ver. 4), or heretical Jewish Christians who taught the necessity of the *circumcision* for *all*, and made use of the name of James without any authority from him; for Peter would not have permitted such men to influence his conduct. Yet they were strict and extremely conservative Jewish Christians who regarded themselves bound to observe the whole law of Moses, without requiring the same from the Gentile converts. This was the position which James himself took at the Council (Acts xv. 16-21), and to which he always adhered, as we may infer from his advice given to Paul (Acts xxi. 20-25), and also from the accounts of tradition (especially Hegesippus, who represents him as a perfect Jewish saint). It would seem from this passage that, soon after the Council, James sent some esteemed brethren of his congregation to Antioch, not for the purpose of imposing the yoke of ceremonialism upon the Gentile Christians, — for this would have been inconsistent with his speech at the Council and with the synodical letter, — but for the purpose of reminding the Jewish Christians of their duty and recommending them to continue the observance of the divinely appointed and time-honored customs of their fathers which were by no means

law: (1.) before Christ it was alive but not life-giving (*lex viva, sed non vivifica*); (2.) from Christ to the destruction of Jerusalem it was dying but not deadly (*moribunda, sed non mortifera*); (3.) after the destruction of Jerusalem it became dead and deadly (*mortua et mortifera*).

overthrown by the compromise measure adopted at the Council. It is unnecessary therefore to charge him with inconsistency. All we can say is that he stopped half way and never ventured so far as Paul, or even as Peter, who broke through the ceremonial restrictions of their native religion. Confining his labors to Jerusalem and the Jews, James regarded it as his duty to adhere as closely as possible to the old dispensation, in the vain hope of bringing over the nation as a whole to the Christian faith ; while the Apostle of the Gentiles, on the contrary, owed it to his peculiar mission to maintain and defend the liberty of the gospel and the rights of the uncircumcised brethren.

Renan (*St. Paul*, ch. x) asserts without proof that James deliberately organized a Jewish counter-mission and sent delegates to the Gentile churches for the purpose of undermining Paul's influence and demanding circumcision as a condition of church membership. This view is as wild as the heretical romance of the Pseudo-Clementine Homilies, and in flat contradiction with the public position and profession of James at the Council (Acts xv.), and his conduct towards Paul, whom he recognized as a brother and fellow-Apostle according to Paul's own statement (ver. 9, comp. i. 19). James was conservative and somewhat contracted, but not heretical.

He used to eat (the imperfect indicates the *habit*) **together with the Gentiles,** *i. e.*, Gentile (uncircumcised) Christians. This is the best proof from the pen of Paul himself that Peter agreed with him in principle, and for a time even in practice. With his accustomed ardor Peter carried out his conviction which he had boldly professed in Jerusalem, and made common cause with the Gentile converts. The Pharisees reproved Christ for eating with sinners (Luke xv. 2). The Jews were strictly forbidden to eat with unclean persons and idolaters. The Gentiles made no distinction between clean and unclean animals, and consumed without scruple the meat offered to idols and sold on the market. The Apostle probably refers here not only to the ordinary meals, but also to the primitive love feasts (agapæ) and the holy communion. A common participation of the Lord's Supper was the completion and seal of Christian-fellowship and church union. We may say that it followed as a last consequence from the decree of the Apostolic Council, but it was not expressly enjoined, and the strict Jewish party thought it unsafe, for the present at least, to venture so far, contenting itself with a general recognition of the Gentile brethren, and keeping them at a respectful distance. James probably shared in this opinion, and may have considered Peter too hasty. The same scrupulous conservatism and exclusivism exists to this day in various shapes of close-communism which refuses to sit at the Lord's table with Christians of any other sect, on account of some difference of doctrine or polity or ceremonies. — **He withdrew and separated himself.** 'The words describe forcibly the cautious withdrawal of a timid person who shrinks from observation.' Characteristic for Peter, who was the first to confess Christ, and the first to deny him ; the first to recognize the rights of the Gentiles, and the first to disown them practically. His strength and weakness, his boldness and timidity are the two opposite manifestations of the same warm, impulsive and impressible temper. He was, like the Galatians, 'liable to

sudden transitions from fever-heat to fever-chill ' (Macgregor). But he was always ready to confess his sins and to repent. And this redeeming feature makes one sympathize with him in his weakness. There was a great deal of human nature in him, but also a great deal of divine grace which triumphed at last. Blameworthy as he was for his inconsistency, he is still more praiseworthy for the humility with which he bore the sharp rebuke of a younger colleague, and lovingly commended the Epistles of 'brother Paul' in which his own inconsistency is recorded (2 Pet. iii. 15, 16). — **Fearing those of the circumcision,** Jewish converts.

Ver. 13. **The other Jews,** *i. e.*, Jewish Christians of Antioch, who very naturally suffered themselves to be carried away by the example and the high authority of Peter. — **Dissembled likewise with him,** were guilty of the same hypocrisy. A very strong, yet truthful expression. For we have here no mere accommodation to weak brethren for the sake of charity and peace, such as Paul himself taught and practised (1 Cor. ix. 20 ; Rom. xiv. 1 ; xv. 3 ; Acts xvi. 3), but a duplicity and self-contradiction at the expense of truth, a denial of the better conviction to the detriment of the Gentile Christians whom Peter acknowledged as brethren in theory, and whom he now disowned in practice. The logical tendency of this conduct was evidently to break up the communion of the two branches of the church, although he himself would no doubt have deplored such a result. — **Even Barnabas,** my friend and co-laborer in the work of heathen missions, and fellow champion of the liberty of the Gentile brethren. This shows the gravity of the crisis and the power of old Jewish habits even upon more liberal minds. The word *even* implies sadness arising from respect and affection. Comp. Cæsar's *Et tu, Brute!* The two friends separated on this occasion, and each pursued an independent path (Acts xv. 39), thus dividing and doubling the work of mission, but Paul afterwards respectfully alludes to Barnabas (1 Cor. ix. 6), and to Mark, his cousin (Col. iv. 16).

Ver. 14. **Straight,** uprightly, honestly. **According to** (the rule of) **the truth.** Others, 'towards,' *i. e.*, so as to maintain the truth of the gospel (comp. ver. 5). — **Before all,** *i. e.*, the assembled congregation. For only in this public way the censure could have its desired effect upon the body of the Jewish Christians. 'A public scandal could not be privately cured' (Jerome). (Comp. 1 Tim. v. 20.)

The following verses to the end of the chapter are a summary report or dramatic sketch of Paul's address to Peter. Vers. 15 to 18 are certainly addressed to Peter, but the personal and historical narrative imperceptibly loses itself in appropriate doctrinal reflections suggested by the occasion and admirably adapted to the case of the Galatians, who had fallen into the same error. In the third chapter it naturally expands into a direct attack on the Galatians. A similar mingling of narrative and reflection occurs in John iii. 14-21, 31-36. — **Livest as the Gentiles,** according to the manner and custom of the Gentiles in regard to eating (ver. 12). The present tense 'livest,' or 'art wont to live,' implies habit and principle (for Peter had partaken of unclean food long before, and by divine command, Acts x. 10-16, 28 ; xi. 3), and brings out more vividly the inconsistency of Peter, who in the same breath gave up his native Judaism and led the Gentile converts back to Judaism. — **Why art thou constraining** (or, **compelling**), not physically and directly, but morally and indirectly, by the force of example which is powerful for good or evil according to the character and position of the man who sets it. It is not necessary to suppose that the delegates of James required from the Gentile converts the observance of the Jewish law of meats. James himself, at all events, confined it to Jewish Christians. But the example of such an Apostle as Peter implied a sort of moral compulsion even for Gentile Christians. — **To Judaize**, to imitate and adopt Jewish manners, to conform to the Jewish religion, without becoming a full Jew. Comp. *Romanize, Romanizing tendency.*

Ver. 15. Many commentators close here the speech of Paul to Peter; others with ver. 16; still others with ver. 18. But the words, '**we** *who are Jews* **by** nature,' would not suit the Galatians, most of whom were Gentiles by birth, and there is no mark of a return of the speech to the Galatians till iii. 1. — **We Jews by birth, and not sinners,** *i. e.,* gross sinners without law and without God, like the heathen. The two words were almost synonymous in the mouth of the Jew. Comp. Matt. ix. 13; Luke vii. 34; Rom. ii. 12; Eph. ii. 12.

Ver. 16. **Yet knowing that a man is not justified by works of law** (law-works, *Gesetzeswerke*), **but only through faith in Jesus Christ, we ourselves also became believers in Christ Jesus.** Here the term 'justify' is first introduced in this Epistle. On the important doctrine of justification see the Excursus below, and the comments on Rom. i. 17 and iii. 20. It means acquittal from the guilt and punishment of sin in the tribunal of the just and holy God, on the ground of Christ's atoning death and through the medium of faith by which we apprehend Christ's merits and make his righteousness our own. 'By works of law,' the whole law, moral as well as ceremonial. — **Shall no flesh be justified,** lit., 'shall all flesh not be justified,' or 'find no justification.' An expressive Hebraism. The negation attaches to the verb, and not to the noun. But the genius of the English language requires such a transposition. 'Flesh' in Hebrew is often used for man, living being. The future tense expresses moral impossibility: such a thing can never happen. The passage is an authoritative confirmation of his own statement by an allusion to Ps. cxliii. 2 : 'Enter not into judgment with Thy servant: for in Thy sight *shall no man living be justified.*' Comp. Rom. iii. 20, where the passage is quoted in the same form with the same addition 'of works of law.'

Vers. 17-19 furnish an example of the condensed and nervous dialectics of Paul, similar to Rom. iii. 3-8. The sense is somewhat obscured by brevity, and has been differently explained. Some make Paul reason from *false* premises of the Judaizers, by drawing from them a logical inference which they themselves must repel with pious horror. But he rather draws, in the form of a question, a false conclusion of the Judaizing opponents from *correct* premises of his own, and rejects their conclusion with his usual formula of abhorrence; just as in Rom. vi. 2 he repels a false antinomian inference from his correct doctrine of justification by faith : 'Shall we continue in sin that grace may abound? God forbid!' His argument is this : But (you may object) if by

seeking gratuitous justification in Christ we had to abandon legal justification and sink to the level of common ' sinners ' (that is, take our position with the profane heathen who know not the law, and can only be justified by faith), does it not follow then (ἄρα) that Christ instead of abolishing sin, promotes sin? Away with this monstrous and blasphemous thought! On the contrary, there is sin in returning to the law after having abandoned it for faith in Christ (as Peter did). I myself (Paul now politely chooses the first person, but means Peter) stand convicted of transgression if I build up again (as thou doest now at Antioch) the very law of Moses which I pulled down (as thou didst at Cæsarea by divine command, and at first in Antioch), and thus condemn my own former conduct. For the law itself taught me to exchange it for Christ to whom it points and leads as a schoolmaster. It would be sin therefore to return to it for justification.

Ver. 17. **Were found,** discovered, in the eyes of God and men, at the time of our conversion to Christ and our justification by faith in him. — **Sinners** in the Jewish sense, *i. e.,* lawless heathen, as in ver. 15. — **A minister of sin,** helper, promoter. — **Let it never be!** or 'Far be it;' 'By no means;' 'Away with the thought;' 'Nay, verily.' This phrase occurs fourteen times in St. Paul, thrice in Galatians (ii. 17, 21; iii. 21), ten times in Romans (iii. 4, 6, 31; vi. 2, 15; vii. 7, 13; ix. 14; xi. 1, 11), and once in 1 Cor. vi. 15. It is an expression of strong denial, often mixed with moral indignation or aversion, and is here and generally used by Paul interjectionally in rebutting an unjustifiable inference deduced from his teaching by an opponent. The rendering ' God forbid ' in the E. V. in all these passages is strongly idiomatic, but unfortunate, as it implies a familiar use of God's name then prevalent in England, which borders on profanity. There is neither 'God' nor 'forbid' in the Greek phrase.

Ver. 18. The sin is the other way, in going back from Christ to Moses, from the gospel of freedom to the law of bondage. Paul speaks with delicate consideration in the first person, but really means Peter and the Judaizers. He supposes a case which actually occurred, and exposes its folly. Peter in this case proved himself an architect of ruin. — **The things which I pulled down,** the Mosaic ordinances, in this case the Levitical law of meats. Paul frequently uses the metaphor of building; comp. 1 Cor. iii. 10-14; 2 Cor. v. 1; x. 4; Rom. xv. 20; Eph. ii. 20-22. — **I prove myself to be a transgressor** of the law itself, by rebuilding it on the ruins of the gospel contrary to its own spirit and intent to prepare the way for the gospel as its fulfillment.

Ver. 19. **For I through law died to law** (a dative of disadvantage) **that I might live to God** (dative of advantage). The same idea is expressed in Rom. vii. 4-6; Col. ii. 20. Paul gives here, in a single sentence, the substance of his own experience, which he more fully explains in the seventh chapter of Romans. The " I " is here Paul himself, and not Peter (as in ver. 18). The law itself led him to Christ, so that it would be sinful and foolish to return to it again, as Peter did. As well might a freedman become a slave, or a man return to childhood. The law is a schoolmaster to lead to Christ (Gal. iii. 24), by developing the sense of sin and the need of redemption. But the very object of a schoolmaster is to elevate the pupil above the need of his instruction and tuition. His success in teaching emancipates the pupil. So children nurse at their mother's breast, that they may outgrow it, and by passing through the school of parental authority and discipline they attain to age, freedom, and independence. The ' law ' is therefore to be taken in the same sense in both cases of the Mosaic law. Comp. Rom. vii. 6-13. Those who (with many of the fathers, and even Luther and Bengel) refer it in the first clause to the law of Christ (Rom. viii. 2), and in the second clause to the law of Moses, miss the drift and beauty of the passage. ' Law ' without the article has a wider sense, and is applicable to all kinds of law, as a general rule or principle, but chiefly and emphatically to the Mosaic law, which is usually indicated by the definite article. — **That I might live unto God,** a new life of obedience to the law of Christ, and gratitude for the redeeming mercy of God. The death of the old man of sin is followed by the resurrection of the new man of righteousness. This cuts off all forms of antinomianism.

Ver. 20. **I have been crucified with Christ** (not ' *am* crucified,' as the E. V. has it). Paul means the past act which took place in his conversion. It is an explanation of the word ' *died*,' ver. 19 (not ' *am dead*,' E. V.). Since the law is a schoolmaster to Christ who fulfilled it and removed its curse by His atoning death on the cross, the believer is crucified with Christ as to his old, sinful nature, but only in order to live a new spiritual life with the risen Saviour. Comp. Rom. vi. 5-10 ; Gal. v. 24 ; vi. 14; Col. ii. 20. **And it is no longer I that live,** or, ' I live no longer myself,' in the unconverted state, under the dominion of sin and the curse of the law. ' I have no longer a separate existence, I am merged in Christ' (Lightfoot). The E. V.: ' *Nevertheless I live, yet not I*,' conveys a beautiful and true idea, but is grammatically incorrect, since the original has no ' nevertheless ' nor ' yet.' — **But it is Christ that liveth in me,** Christ, the crucified and risen Redeemer, who is the resurrection and the life, is the indwelling, animating, and controlling principle of my life. One of the strongest and clearest passages for the precious doctrine of a real life-union of Christ with the believer, as distinct both from a mere moral union and sympathy, and from a pantheistic confusion and mixture. Christ truly lives and moves in the believer, but the believer lives and moves also, as a self-conscious personality, in Christ. Faith is the bond which so unites the soul to Christ, that it puts on Christ (iii. 27), that it becomes a member of His body, yea flesh of His flesh and bone of His bone (Eph. v. 30), and derives all its spiritual nourishment from

Him (John xv. 1 ff.). Comp. Gal. iii. 27 : ' Ye did put on Christ;' iv. 19: ' Until Christ be formed in you ;' 2 Cor. i. 3, 5 : ' Jesus Christ is in you ;' Col. iii. 4 : ' When Christ who is our life, shall appear ;' Phil. i. 21 : ' For to me to live is Christ ;' John xv. 5 : ' I am the vine, ye are the branches ;' John xvii. 23 : ' I in them, and Thou in Me, that they may be perfected into one.' — **That** (life) **which I now live in the flesh.** 'Now' after my conversion, as compared with my old life. ' In the flesh,' in this bodily, temporal form of existence. It is explanatory of the preceding sentence. The life-union with Christ does not destroy the personality of the believer. Even his natural mortal life continues in this world, but as the earthen vessel containing the heavenly treasure of the imperishable life of Christ who dwells in him and transforms even the body into a temple of the Holy Spirit. — **I live in the faith,** (not ' *by*,' E. V.) corresponds to ' in the flesh,' and conveys the idea that faith is the living element in which Paul moved. — **Of the Son of God,** the object of faith, the eternal Son of the Father who has life in himself (John v. 26), and by his incarnation and his atoning death on the cross has become the fountain of divine life to man. — **Who loved me,** individually, as a personal friend. The love of Christ to the whole world applies in its full force to each believing soul, as the sun pours its whole light and heat with undiminished force on every object it reaches.

Ver. 21. **I do not frustrate,** or set at nought, make of no effect, nullify, as the Judaizers do with their assertion of the necessity of the law for justification. — **The grace of God,** which revealed itself in the infinite love and atoning death of Christ, ver. 20. — **Christ died** (not ' is dead,' E. V.) **for nought,** or ' uselessly,' ' gratuitously,' *i. e.*, without good cause ; not ' in vain ' (*i. e.*, without fruit or effect). If the observance of the law of Moses or any other human work could justify and save man, the atoning death of Christ would be unnecessary as well as fruitless. This blasphemous inference gives the finishing stroke to the false Judaizing gospel.

The power of this concluding argument Peter could not resist, and he no' doubt felt ashamed and humbled at this overwhelming rebuke, as he did after the denial of his Master, although Paul, from discretion and kindness, says nothing of the result of this collision. The effect of it was long felt : to the Ebionites it furnished material for an attack upon Paul, to the Gnostics for an attack upon the Jewish apostles, to Porphyry for an attack upon Christianity itself. But Christianity has survived all these attacks, and gains new strength from every conflict.

Excursus on the Controversy of Peter and Paul.

CHAPTER II. 11-14.

The collision of the two Apostles was of course only temporary. Peter showed weakness, Paul rebuked him, Peter submitted, and both continued to labor, at a respectful distance, yet as brethren (comp. 1 Cor. ix. 5 ; 2 Pet. iiL 15, 16), for their common Master until they sealed their testimony by their blood and met again never more to part in the church triumphant above. The same is true of the alienation of Paul from Barnabas and Mark, which took place about the same time, but was adjusted afterwards, as we learn from Paul's respectful allusion to Barnabas (1 Cor. ix. 6), and Mark's later connection with Paul (Col. iv. 10; Philem. 24; 2 Tim. iv. 11).[1] At the same time it cannot be denied that the scene in Antioch reveals an immense fermentation and commotion in the Apostolic Church, which was not a dead unit, but a living process and a struggle of conflicting views and tendencies with an underlying harmony. On the one hand the quarrel has been greatly exaggerated by Celsus, Porphyry, and other enemies of Christianity, old and new, who used it as a weapon against the character and inspiration of the Apostles; on the other hand it has been explained away and dishonestly misinterpreted by eminent fathers and Roman commentators in mistaken zeal for a rigid and mechanical orthodoxy.

We take the record in its natural, historical sense, and derive from it the following instructive lessons : —

1. The right and duty of protest against ecclesiastical authority, even the highest, when Christian truth and principle are endangered. The protest should be manly, yet respectful. Paul was no doubt severe, but yet he recognized Peter expressly as a 'pillar' of the Church and a brother in Christ (Gal. i. 18; ii. 9). There was no personal bitterness and rudeness, as we find, alas, in the controversial writings of St. Jerome (against Rufinus), St. Bernard (against Abelard), Luther (against Erasmus and Zwingli), Bossuet (against Fenelon), and other great divines.

2. The duty to subordinate expediency to principle, the favor of man to the truth of God. Paul himself recommended and practised charity to the weak ; but here a fundamental right, the freedom in Christ, was at stake, which Peter compromised by his conduct, after he himself had manfully stood up for the true principle at the Council of Jerusalem, and for the liberal practice at Antioch before the arrival of the Judaizers.

3. The moral imperfection of the Apostles. They remained even after the Pentecostal illumination frail human beings, carrying the heavenly treasure in earthen vessels, and stood in daily need of forgiveness (2 Cor. iv. 7; Phil. iii. 12; James iii. 2; 1 John i. 8; ii. 2). The weakness of Peter is here recorded, as his greater sin of denying his Lord is recorded in the Gospels, both for the warning and for the comfort of believers. If the chief of the Apostles was led astray, how much more should ordinary Christians be on their guard against temptation! But if Peter found remission, we may confidently expect the same on the same condition of hearty repentance. 'The dissension — if dissension it could be called — between the two great Apostles will shock those only who, in defiance of all Scripture, persist in regarding the Apostles as specimens of supernatural perfection.' (Farrar, Life and Work of St. Paul, i. 444.)

4. The collision does not justify any unfavorable conclusion against the inspiration of the Apostles and the infallibility of their teaching. For Paul charges his colleague with hypocrisy or dissimulation, that is, with acting against his own better conviction. We have here a fault of conduct, a temporary inconsistency, not a permanent error of doctrine. A man may know and teach the truth, and yet go astray occasionally in practice. Peter had the right view of the relation of the gospel to the Gentiles ever since the conversion of Cornelius; he openly defended it at the Apostolic Council (Acts xv. 7; comp. Gal. ii. 1-9), and never renounced it in theory; on the contrary, his own Epistles agree fully with those of Paul, and are in part addressed to the same Galatians with a view to confirm them in their Pauline faith; but he suffered himself to be influenced by some scrupulous and contracted Jewish Christians from Jerusalem. By trying to please one party he offended the other, and endangered for a moment the sound doctrine itself.

5. The inconsistency here rebuked quite agrees with Peter's character as it appears in the Gospels. The same impulsiveness and inconstancy of temper, the same mixture of boldness and timidity, made him the first to confess, and the first to deny Christ, the strongest and the weakest among the Twelve. He refused that Christ should wash his feet, and then by a sudden change he wished not his feet only, but his hands and head to be washed; he cut off the ear of Malchus, and in a few minutes afterwards he forsook his Master and fled; he solemnly promised to be faithful to Him, though all should forsake Him, and yet in the same night he denied Him thrice. If the legend of Domine quo vadis (which is first mentioned in the Apocryphal Acts of Peter and Paul) has any foundation in fact, he remained 'consistently inconsistent' to the last. A few days before his execution, it is said, he escaped from prison, but when he reached a spot outside of Rome, near the gate of St. Sebastian, now marked by a chapel, the Lord appeared to him with a cross, and Peter asked in surprise : 'Lord, whither goest thou?' (Domine, quo vadis ?) And when the Lord replied : 'I am going to Rome to be crucified again,' the disciple returned deeply humbled, and delivered himself to the jailor to be crucified head downwards.

6. It should be remembered, however, on the other hand, first, that the question concerning the significance of the Mosaic law, and especially of the propriety of eating meat offered to idols, was a very difficult one and continued to be agitated in the Apostolic Church (comp. 1 Cor. viii.-x.; Rom. xiv.). The decree of the Council at Jerusalem (Acts xv. 20, 29), after all, stated simply the duties of the Gentile converts, strictly prohibiting them the use of meat offered to idols, but it said nothing on the duties of the Jewish Christians to the former, thus leaving some room for a milder and stricter view on the subject. We should also remember that the temptation on the occasion referred to was very great, since even Barnabas, the Gentile missionary, was overcome by it.

7. Much as we may deplore and censure the weakness of Peter and admire the boldness and consistency of Paul, the humility and meekness with which Peter, the oldest and most eminent of the twelve Apostles, seems to have borne the public rebuke of a younger colleague, are deserving of high praise. How touching is his subsequent allusion in 2 Pet. iii. 15, 16, which is addressed to the

---

[1] The words used by Luke of the general controversy in the Council at Jerusalem (Acts xv. 2), are στάσις (dissension, a factious party spirit) and ζήτησις (disputation, questioning) ; the word used of the quarrel between Paul and Barnabas (xv. 39), is παροξυσμός, exacerbatio, paroxysm, and implies a warm and sharp contentiou, heightened in this case by the previous friendship and coöperation, yet, after all, passing away as a temporary alienation. The same word is used Heb. x. 24 in a good sense of 'provocation to love and good works'

Galatians among others, to the very Epistles of his 'beloved brother Paul,' in one of which his own conduct is so sharply condemned. This required a rare degree of divine grace which did its full work in him through much suffering and humiliation, as the humble, meek, gentle, and graceful spirit of his Epistles abundantly proves.

8. The conduct of Paul supplies a conclusive argument in favor of the equality of the Apostles and against the papal view of the supremacy of Peter. No pope would or could allow any Catholic bishop or archbishop to call him to an account and to talk to him in that style of manly independence. The conduct of Peter is also fatal to the claim of papal infallibility, as far as morals or discipline is concerned ; for Peter acted here officially with all the power of his Apostolic example, and however correct in doctrine, he erred very seriously in practice, and endangered the great principle of Christian freedom, as the popes have done ever since. No wonder that the story was offensive to some of the fathers and Roman commentators, and gave rise to most unnatural explanations.

We may add that the account of the Council in Jerusalem in Acts xv. likewise contradicts the Vatican system, which would have required a reference of the great controversy on circumcision to the Apostle Peter rather than to a council under the presidency of James.

9. The Apostolic Church is typical and foreshadows the whole course of the history of Christendom. Peter, Paul, and John represent as many ages and phases of the Church. Peter is the rock of Catholicism, Paul the rock of evangelical Protestantism. Their temporary collision at Antioch anticipates the world-historical antagonism of Romanism and Protestantism, which continues to this day. It is an antagonism between legal bondage and evangelical freedom, between Judaizing conservatism and Christian progress. Jerusalem, Rome, and Petersburg are in different degrees on the side of Peter; Wittenberg, Geneva, and Oxford—at various distances and with temporary reactions—follow the standard of Paul. Let us hope also for a future reconciliation in the ideal Church of harmony and peace which is symbolized by John, the bosom friend of Christ, the seer of the heavenly Jerusalem.

Paul and Peter, as far as we know from the New Testament, never met again after this scene in Antioch. But ecclesiastical tradition reports that they were tried and condemned together in Rome, and executed on the same day (the 29th of June), Peter, the Galilæan disciple, on the hill of the Janiculum, where he was crucified ; Paul, the Roman citizen, on the Ostian road at the Tre Fontane, where he was beheaded. Their martyr blood thus mingled is still a fountain of life to the church of God.

Excursus on Justification.

CHAPTER II. 16, 17.

The doctrine of justification by faith is one of the fundamental doctrines of Paul, and is set forth most fully in this Epistle and in that to the Romans. How shall a sinner be justified before a holy God? This was a vital question in the Apostolic age, and came very near splitting the Church. It shook Western Christendom again in the sixteenth century, and divided it into two camps. It is no idle scholastic dispute, but involves the peace of conscience and affects man's whole conduct. It is nearly equivalent to the question : ' What shall I do to be saved?'

To this question there were two answers. The Pharisaical Jews and Christian Judaizers said : ' Man is justified by works of the law.' Paul said just as emphatically : ' Man is justified by faith in Christ.' The Judaizers would not deny the importance and necessity of faith in Christ, but practically they laid the main stress upon works, and hence they demanded circumcision as a term of church membership, and a sign and pledge for the observance of the whole Mosaic law. Paul reasons in this chapter that to return to the law for justification is virtually to abandon Christ, and to declare his death needless and fruitless.

The following are the chief points to be considered here : —

1. The verb to justify (δικαιόω) may be used both in an efficient and in a judicial sense, i. e., (1.) to make just, to transform a sinner into a saint ; (2.) to declare just, to acquit. In Hellenistic Greek, and especially in Paul's Epistles, it has the judicial or forensic meaning. This appears —

(a.) From the equivalent terms ' to reckon,' or ' to account for righteousness.' Gal. iii. 6; Rom. iv. 3, 5, 9, 23, 24 ; James ii. 23.

(b.) From the phrase to be justified ' before God,' or ' in the sight of God,' i. e., before His tribunal. Gal. iii. 11 ; Rom. iii. 20.

(c.) From such passages where God or Christ is said to be justified. God is just and cannot be made just, but He may be accounted or declared just by man. Rom. iii. 4 (from Ps. li. 4) ; 1 Tim. iii. 16; comp. Matt. xi. 19 ; Luke vi. 29, 35.

(d.) From the opposite phrase to condemn. Matt. xii. 37 : ' By thy words shalt thou be justified, and by thy words shalt thou be condemned ;' Deut. xxv. 1 : ' The judges shall justify the righteous and condemn the wicked ;' Prov. xvii. 15.

2. Consequently ' justification ' (δικαίωσις, Rom. iv. 25 ; v. 18) is a judicial act of acquittal, in opposition to condemnation.

Now there may be two kinds of justification, legal and evangelical. The former would be a reward of merit, the latter a free gift of grace. We may be justified and accepted by God on the ground of our good works, the observance of His law, that is, because we are really righteous and deserving of acceptance ; or we may be justified gratuitously on the ground of the merits of Christ the righteous, as apprehended by a living faith.

But justification by works is impossible, because we are all sinners by nature and practice, and justly exposed to the wrath of God. We cannot in our own strength observe the divine law; if we could, there would have been no need of a Saviour and his death to atone for our sins. The more we try to keep the law, the more are we driven to a conviction of sin and guilt and to a painful sense of the need of redemption. This is the pedagogic or educational mission of the law. It is in itself 'holy, just, and good,' but it is opposed and defeated by the power of sin in the flesh, or the corrupt nature of man, which it cannot overcome. It is therefore no 'quickening spirit,' but a 'killing letter.' The best it can do is to bring the moral decease to a crisis by revealing sin in its true nature, and thus to prepare the way for the cure.[1]

3. Hence we are shut up to gratuitous justification by the free grace of God through faith in Christ who came into the world for the very purpose of redeeming us from the curse of the law and the guilt and power of sin. God is the judge; we stand charged before His tribunal with violation of his holy law; Christ steps in with his merits as our surety; we accept Him as our Saviour, in sincere repentance and faith; God pronounces us just for His son's sake, pardons our sins and adopts us as His children. This is justification as taught by Paul. The atoning death of Christ is the meritorious ground of our justification; a living faith in Him is the condition on our part; a holy obedience is the evidence or necessary consequence.

4. For it is impossible truly to believe in Christ without following his example. We are not justified outside of Christ, but in Christ, standing in Him, united with Him, identified with Him, consecrated to Him. Faith without works is dead. Paul demands a faith which is 'operative by love' (Gal. v. 16). He insists on good works fully as much as his Judaizing opponents, but as a result of justification, not as a condition of it. The truly good works are works of faith and manifestations of gratitude to God for his redeeming love in Christ. Paul only carried out the teaching of Christ who attributes saving power not to love or hope or works of men, but to faith. 'Thy faith hath saved thee;' 'He that believeth in Me hath (already here and now) eternal life.' In all these cases faith is not merely a theoretical belief, but trust of the heart, repose of the will in Christ, an outgoing of the whole inner man towards Him as our Saviour. Faith is the bond of a vital union with Christ and appropriates his righteousness and all his benefits. 'It is a living, busy, active, mighty power, and cannot possibly cease from working good.' The same grace of God which justifies, does also regenerate and sanctify. Faith and love, justification and sanctification are as inseparable in the life of the true Christian as light and heat in the rays of the sun.

Paul's doctrine of justification then differs as widely from antinomianism which denies the necessity of good works, as it differs from Jewish legalism, and all its kindred errors which make good works an antecedent condition of justification and virtually teach that man is his own Saviour.

5. Paul's doctrine of justification is a source of unspeakable comfort and peace. It humbles our pride, it gives us a full assurance of pardon, it fills us with a deep sense of the boundless love of God, and the all-sufficient salvation of Christ. It acts as the strongest stimulus of gratitude and entire consecration to the service of Him who loved us and gave Himself for us.

CHAPTER III.

The Justification by Faith, and the Curse of the Law.

Chapter III. 1-14.

Paul addresses himself again directly to the Galatians with an expression of his indignant surprise at the folly of their relapse into Judaism, and passes from the historical to the doctrinal part of the Epistle, from the apology of his apostolic authority to the defence of his apostolic teaching concerning justification by faith and evangelical freedom, in opposition to the slavish legalism which would make Christ's death superfluous and useless. He first reminds the readers of their own experience which must teach them that they received the Holy Spirit not through the law, but through faith (vers. 1-5); and then he appeals to the example of Abraham who was justified by faith, and whose genuine children are those who believe like him (vers. 6-9). The law on the contrary pronounces the curse upon every transgressor, and cannot possibly justify any man, since they are all transgressors (vers. 10-12). Christ alone by His atoning death delivered us from this curse (vers. 13, 14).

---

[1] Milton has a striking passage (*Parad. Lost*, xii. 285) in illustration of Paul's doctrine :—

'And therefore Law was given them to *evince*
Their *natural pravity*, by stirring up
Sin against Law to fight; that when they see
Law can discover sin, but not remove,
Save by those shadowy expiations weak,
The blood of bulls and goats, they may conclude
Some blood more precious must be paid for man.'

1 O FOOLISH Galatians, *a* who hath [1] bewitched you, that
ye should not *b* obey the truth,[2] before whose eyes Jesus
Christ hath been evidently set forth, *c* crucified among you? [3]

2 This only would I learn of you, Received ye *d* the Spirit by the

3 works of the law,[4] *e* or by the hearing [5] of faith? Are ye so
foolish? *f* having begun in the Spirit, are ye now made perfect

4 by *g* the flesh? [6] *h* Have ye suffered [7] so many things in vain?

5 if *it be* yet [8] in vain.   He therefore *i* that ministereth to you
the Spirit, and worketh miracles among you,[9] *doeth he it* [10] by
the works of the law,[11] or by the hearing [12] of faith?

6 Even as *k* 'Abraham believed God, and it was accounted [13]

7 to him for righteousness.' Know ye [14] therefore that *l* they
which [15] are of faith, the same are the children [16] of Abraham.

8 And *m* the Scripture, foreseeing that God would justify the
heathen [17] through faith, preached before the gospel [18] unto

9 Abraham, *saying,* *n* 'In thee shall all nations [19] be blessed.' So
then they which be [20] of faith are blessed with [21] faithful Abraham.

10 For as many as are of the works of the law [22] are under
the [23] curse: for it is written, *o* 'Cursed *is* every one that continueth not in all things which are written in the book of the

11 law to do them.' But *p* that no man is justified by the law [24]
in the sight of God, *it* [25] *is* evident: for, *q* 'The just [26] shall live

12 by faith.' And *r* the law is not of faith: but, *s* 'The man that

13 doeth them [27] shall live in them.' *t* Christ hath [28] redeemed us
from the curse of the law, being made [29] a curse for us: for it
is written, *u* 'Cursed *is* every one that hangeth on a tree:'

14 *v* That the blessing of Abraham might come on the Gentiles
through [30] Jesus Christ; that we might receive *w* the promise of
the Spirit through faith.

a Chap. v. 7;
comp. Acts
b viii. 9, 11.
Chap. v. 7.
c 1 Cor. i. 2, 3;
ii. 2.
d Ver. 14;
Acts ii. 38;
viii. 15; x.
47; xv. 8;
Eph. i. 13;
Heb. vi. 4.
e Ver. 5;
Rom. x. 16,
17.
f Chap. iv. 9;
Phil. i. 6.
g Heb. vii. 16;
ix. 10.
h Heb. x. 35,
36; 2 John
8.
i 2 Cor. iii. 8.
k Gen. xv. 6;
Rom. iv. 3,
9, 21, 22;
James ii. 23.
l John viii.
39; Rom.
iv. 11, 12, 16.
m Ver. 22; iv.
30; see
Rom. ix. 17.
n Gen. xii, 3;
xviii. 18;
comp. xxii.
18; Acts iii.
25.
o Deut. xxvii.
26; Jer. xi.
3.
p Chap. ii. 16.
q Hab. ii. 4;
Rom. i. 17;
Heb. x. 38.
r Rom. iv. 4,
5; x. 5, 6;
xi. 6.
s Lev. xviii.
5; Rom. x.
5.
t Chap. iv. 5;
Rom. viii. 3;
2 Cor. v. 21;
2 Pet. ii. 1.
u Deut. xxi.
23.
v Rom. iv. 9,
16.
w Acts ii. 33;
Is. xxxii. 15;
xlvi. 3; Jer.
xxxi. 33;
xxxii. 40;
Ez. xi. 19;
xxxvi. 27;
Joel ii. 28,
29; Zech.
xii. 10;
John vii. 39.

[1] *omit* hath
[2] *The best authorities omit the words* that ye should not obey the truth.
(*Probably a gloss from chap.* v. 7.)
[3] was openly set forth among you, as crucified. (*Some of the best MSS.
omit* among you.)   [4] Did ye receive the Spirit by works of law?
[5] preaching (message)   [6] are ye now ending (finishing) in the flesh?
[7] Did ye experience   [8] if it be really (indeed)   [9] powers in you
[10] *doth he do so*   [11] by works of law   [12] preaching   [13] reckoned
[14] Ye perceive (*indicative*)   [15] those who   [16] sons
[17] God justifieth the Gentiles   [18] declared beforehand the good tidings
[19] all the Gentiles   [20] those who are   [21] *insert* the
[22] of works of law (law-works)   [23] *omit* the   [24] *lit.* in law (by law)
[25] *omit* it   [26] *Or,* the righteous
[27] He that hath done them (*i. e. observed the commandments*)
[28] *omit* hath   [29] by becoming   [30] in

Ver. 1. **O senseless Galatians**, to think that righteousness comes through the law, and thus virtually to deny the necessity and efficacy of Christ's death (ii. 21). No reference to natural dullness or stupidity (for the Galatians, like all the Celtic races, were bright and intelligent), but to spiritual folly. The same word is used by our Lord of the disciples of Emmaus (Luke xxiv. 25). — **Did bewitch you**, fascinate with his evil eye. The relapse from the freedom of the gospel to the slavery of the law is so absurd that it seems only explicable on the assumption of magical agency. The Greek word (βασκάνειν), originally referred to witchery by spells or incantations, then to the blighting influence of the evil eye (especially on children), according to a common belief still prevalent in Egypt and throughout the East, also in Italy ('occhio cattivo'), and among the Celts in Brittany. It implies the envious spirit of the false teachers and their baleful influence on the Galatians.[1] — **Before whose eyes Jesus Christ was evidently** (or, **conspicuously**) **set forth**. This signifies the life-like, pictorial vivacity, and effectiveness of Paul's preaching of Christ and Him crucified, who by his death delivered us from the curse and slavery of the law and reconciled us to God. The Greek verb is used of placarding public notices and proclamations. More freely we might translate: 'You, before whose very eyes was held up the picture of Jesus Christ on the cross.' Faithful preaching is the best painting. Paul intimates that the actual sight of Christ's death could not have affected them more powerfully than his preaching. 'When the church has such painters, she needs no longer dead images of wood and stone.' (Calvin). — **Among you**, lit. 'in you' (omitted by some of the best editors) may be connected either with the verb 'set forth,' as a redundant phrase (not only by letter from a distance, but by my own personal presence and preaching), or with 'crucified,' in this sense: The crucifixion has been so graphically described to you as if it had occurred in the midst of you and in your very hearts. The former is preferable on account of the order of words. — **Crucified** is emphatically placed at the end, as in 1 Cor. i. 23 : 'We preach Christ, and him crucified,' and 1 Cor. ii. 2. The perfect participle implies the permanent character and result of the crucifixion. Christ crucified is the greatest conqueror, and draws all hearts to him. Comp. John xii. 32.

Ver. 2. Paul appeals to their own experience at their conversion, which alone should be sufficient to convince them of the error of their present position. **This only**, among other concessions which I might draw from your own spiritual experience. The 'only' indicates that this is sufficient. **Was it by works of law** (law-works, *Gesetzeswerke*) **that ye received the Spirit**, the Holy Spirit, the greatest of gifts. He is communicated to believers through the gospel, regenerates and sanctifies and makes them children of God and heirs of eternal life. In the apostolic age, the Spirit manifested itself also in extraordinary gifts such as speaking in tongues, prophesying, working of miracles (comp. Acts viii. 17 ; x. 44-46 ; xix. 6 ; 1 Cor. xii.-xiv.) — **From the preaching** (or, **message**,

not 'hearing ') **of faith**, comp. ver. 5; 1 Thess. ii. 13 ; Heb. iv. 2 ; and Rom. x. 17: 'faith cometh from preaching, and preaching through the word of God.' The Greek (ἀκοή) admits of two meanings : (1.) active : the hearing of faith, *i. e.*, the reception of the gospel preached (comp. 'obedience of faith,' Rom. i. 5; xvi. 26) ; (2.) passive : the report, the message which treats of faith (genit. of the object). Lightfoot adopts the first, but the second is preferable on account of the usual meaning of the word in the New Testament, and because the contrast is between the two principles, *law* and *faith*, not between two actions, *doing* and *hearing*. The emphasis lies on 'law' and 'faith.' In the New Testament, 'faith' is mostly used in the subjective sense of the act and exercise of faith, not in the objective sense of doctrine or creed. Faith is the organ by which we receive the Holy Spirit through the preaching of the gospel.

Ver. 3. **Having begun in the Spirit, are ye now ending** (or **finishing**) **in the flesh?** A fine irony. The middle voice of the Greek verb (ἐπιτελεῖσθε) is preferable to the passive ('are ye now brought to perfection') on account of the correspondence with 'begun,' and on account of the parallel passages, Phil. i. 6 ('he who began a good work in you will finish it '), and 2 Cor. viii. 6. 'Spirit' and 'flesh' represent here the spiritual religion which makes man free, and the carnal religion which makes him a slave to outward forms and observances.

Ver. 4. **Did ye experience so many things in vain?** The usual rendering 'suffer' would refer to persecutions which the Galatians had to endure (probably from the Jews; but as we know nothing of them, it seems preferable to take the Greek verb (ἐπάθετε) in the neutral and wider sense (otherwise not found in the New Testament, except perhaps in Mark v. 26), embracing all spiritual experiences (blessings and benefits as well) of the Galatians (comp. vers. 3 and 5). — **If it be really in vain**. This leaves room for doubt; the Apostle cannot believe that the Galatians will lose all the benefit of their spiritual experiences and continue in their folly. Others take the words in the sense : 'if it be only in vain,' and not much worse ; since spiritual experiences increase the responsibility and risk. Comp. Luke xii. 47, 48 ; 2 Pet. ii. 21.

Ver. 5. The present tense **ministereth** and **worketh** is used to indicate the continued communication and abundant supply of the spiritual gifts. — **Powers**, miraculous powers, 1 Cor. xii. 10, 28, 29. — **In you**, *i. e.*, in your heart and will ; comp. Matt. xiv. 2. Paul probably means the moral miracles of regeneration and conversion. Others understand here physical miracles wrought 'among you,' *i. e.* in the midst of you.

Ver. 6. The only reply the Galatians could make to the foregoing question was : 'By the preaching of faith.' Taking this for granted, Paul proceeds (as in Rom. iv. 1) to give the historical and scriptural proof from the example of Abraham, the father of the faithful. The words are a quotation from Gen. xv. 6 (Sept.). The emphasis lies on **believed**, *i. e.*, trusted in God.

Ver. 7. **Ye perceive, therefore**. The Greek may be the indicative or the imperative. The former agrees better with the argumentative character of the sentence and with the particle 'therefore' (ἄρα). Others maintain that the imperative ('know ye ') is more animated. — **Those of faith**,

[1] Coleridge (*Lady Christabel*) :—

'So deeply had she drunken in
That look, those shrunken serpent eyes,
That all her features were resigned
To this sole image of her mind.'

3

emphatic, no others, in opposition to the self-righteous men of the law. 'They whose starting-point, whose fundamental principle is faith.' Comp. Rom. ii. 8 ; iv. 14 (in Greek).

Ver. 8. **The Scripture,** personified, as in ver. 22, for the author of the Scripture. — **Justifieth,** now when Paul wrote, and at all times. It is the normal present indicating the only way of God's justification, and sure accomplishment of his purpose. — **Declared beforehand the good tidings.** The promise to Abraham was an anticipation of the gospel, *i. e.*, the good tidings of salvation by Christ. — **In thee,** as the spiritual father. Quotation from two passages (Gen. xii. 3, and xviii. 18), which are fused into one. The blessing promised includes the whole Christian salvation, which implies justification, *i e.*, the remission of sins and imputation of Christ's merit.

Ver. 9. The emphasis lies on **faith,** as in ver. 7.

Vers. 10-12. Negative proof of ver. 9, by showing the impossibility of justification by law, because we cannot keep the law, and the violation of the law subjects us to its curse (comp. Rom. iii. 9-20 ; vii. 7-25). No man lives up even to his own imperfect standard of goodness, much less to the perfect rule of the revealed will of the holy God.

Ver. 10 confirms ver. 9 by the opposite. **As many as are of law-works,** are controlled by the principle of law, and shape their character by works, **are under curse,** *i. e.*, subject to curse (comp. 'under sin,' Rom. iii. 9). — **For it is written,** etc. A free quotation from Deut. xxvii. 26 (Sept.), the closing sentence of the curses from Mount Ebal, and a summary of the whole.

Vers. 11 and 12 contain the following syllogism : The just lives by faith ; the law is not of faith : consequently no man is justified by the law.

Ver. 11. **Now that in (the) law no man is justified in the sight of God, is evident.** 'In' is elemental and instrumental, 'in and by,' or 'under' the law, in the sphere and domain of the law. 'In the sight,' in the judgment of God ; man standing as a culprit before His tribunal. **For the righteous shall live by faith.** From Hab. ii. 4, according to the Septuagint. Comp. note to Rom. i. 17. The passage refers originally to the preservation of the righteous Israelite amidst the ruin of the Chaldæan invasion. The stress lays on 'faith,' as the power which gives life. ' By faith' must not be joined with 'righteous,' but with 'shall live'; this is required by the original Hebrew ('the righteous shall live by *his faith*,' or 'his fidelity'), by the rendering of the Septuagint ('the righteous shall live *by my faith*,' or according to another reading : '*my righteous* shall live by faith'), and by the contrast between 'live by faith,' and 'to live in them,' *i. e.*, in the commandments (ver. 12). The Old Testament, then, already declares faith to be the fountain of spiritual life and salvation, or rather the organ by which we apprehend and appropriate the saving grace of God in Christ to our individual use and benefit.

Ver. 12. **The law is not of** [springs not from] **faith, but** [declares], '**He who hath done them**' [*i. e.*, the statutes and judgments, previously mentioned in the Old Testament passage,] '**shall live in them.**' Quotation from Lev. xviii. 5. The life-element of the law is not faith, but work. *Doing*

is the essential thing in law. Faith *receives* the gift of God, the law requires us to *give*, to perform all its enactments.

Ver. 13. **Christ redeemed us from the curse of the law by becoming a curse for us.** One of the strongest passages for the doctrine of a vicarious atonement. Christ, out of infinite love and in full agreement with the Father's eternal plan of redemption, voluntarily assumed, bore and abolished, by His death on the cross, the whole curse of the outraged law in the stead and in behalf of sinners. The vicarious efficacy lies not so much in the preposition 'for,' as in the whole sentence. What He did and suffered for men, He did and suffered in their stead, and what He suffered in their stead, He suffered for their benefit. — ' Redeemed,' delivered (by one act accomplished, once and for all) by a ransom, *i. e.*, Christ's life offered on the cross. Comp. Matt. xx. 28 (He 'gave his life a ransom for many ') ; 1 Tim. ii. 6 ; 1 Cor. v. 20 ; vii. 23 ; Tit. ii. 14 ; Rev. v. 9 ; xiv. 4. — ' By becoming a curse,' stronger, and yet milder than 'accursed.' Christ was the voluntary bearer of the entire guilt of the whole race, yet without any *personal* guilt. The curse is transferred from the guilty sinner to the innocent victim (as in the case of the typical scape-goat. Lev. xvi. s. ff.). Comp. 2 Cor. v. 21 : ' Him [Christ] who knew no sin He [God] made *to be* sin [stronger than sinner] for us (or, on our behalf) ; that we might become the righteousness of God in Him.' — ' For us,' on our behalf, for our sakes. — **For it is written,** etc. A parenthetic justification from Deut. xxi. 23 (Sept.) of the startling expression just used. The passage refers to those criminals who after being stoned were hung up on a stake (probably on the form of a cross), but were not permitted to remain in this position over night, lest the holy land should be desecrated. Our Saviour fulfilled the legal curse by hanging dead on the cross. Paul significantly omits the words ' of God ' which are in the Septuagint and in the Hebrew. For Christ was not Himself accursed of God, but only in a vicarious sense, that is, by the voluntary self-assumption of the curse of others, and in full harmony with the Father's wish and will, who, far from hating his own beloved Son, delighted in His sacrifice on the cross as 'a sweet-smelling savor ' (Eph. v. 2), and in the execution of His own eternal purpose of redeeming mercy. Riddle : ' Two curses are mentioned by Paul. The one : ' Cursed is every one that continueth not,' etc. (ver. 10). That curse lay on all mankind. The other : ' Cursed is every one that hangeth on a tree ' (ver. 13). This curse Christ took that He might redeem us from the first. Both were curses in and of the law. The one specifies the guilt, the other the punishment. Christ bore the accursed punishment, and thus took away the accursed guilt. He stood for the *every one* who continueth not, by becoming the *very one* who hung upon the tree.'

Ver. 14. **The blessing of Abraham,** justification by faith and the whole Messianic salvation. — **We,** *i. e.*, all Christians whether of Jewish or Gentile descent. — **Receive the promise of the Spirit,** refers back to ver. 2. ' After a wondrous chain of arguments, expressed with equal force, brevity, and profundity, the apostle comes back to the subject of ver. 2 ; the gift of the Holy Ghost came through faith in Jesus Christ.' (Ellicott.)

The Educational Mission of the Law.

CHAPTER III. 15-29.

Paul now assumes a milder tone, and reasons with the Galatians from the common dealings of men. Even a human covenant is sacred and cannot be set aside, much more a divine covenant. Hence the promise of God to Abraham and to his seed, *i. e.*, to his believing posterity summed up in Christ, cannot be annulled by the law which came in several hundred years later (vers. 15-18), but the law intervened between the promise and its fulfilment, or between Abraham and Christ as a school of discipline, or as a schoolmaster to prepare men for the freedom in Christ (19-24), so that now by faith in Christ we are no more slaves, but sons and heirs (25-29).

15 BRETHREN, I speak after the manner of men; *a* Though *a* Heb. ix. 17.
   it be but a man's covenant, yet *if it be* confirmed,[1] no man *b* Gen. xii. 7;
16 disannulleth,[2] or addeth thereto.   Now *b* to Abraham and his xiii. 15; xvii. 7, 8.
   seed were the promises made.[3]   He saith not, 'And to seeds,' *c* Gen. xvii. 7; xxii. 18;
   as of many; but as of one, *c* 'And to thy seed,' which is *d* Christ. *d* Acts iii. 25. Comp. vers.
17 And this I say,[4] *that*[5] the[6] covenant, that was confirmed be- 28, 29; I Cor. xii. 12,
   fore of God in Christ,[7] the law, *e* which was[8] four hundred and *e* Ex. xii. 40, 41; Acts
   thirty years after, cannot disannul,[9] *f* that it should make the vii. 6.
18 promise of none effect.[10]   For if *g* the inheritance *be* of the[11] *f* Rom. iv. 13, 14; ver. 21.
   law, *h it is* no more of promise: but God gave[12] *it* to Abra- *g* Rom. viii. 17.
   ham by promise. *h* Rom. iv. 14.
19   Wherefore then *serveth* the law?[13]   *i* It was added[14] because *i* Rom. iv. 15; v. 20; viii. 8, 13; I Tim.
   of[15] transgressions, till *k* the seed should come[16] to whom the i. 9.
   promise was made;[17] *and it was*[18] *l* ordained by[19] angels in[20] *k* Ver. 16.
   l Acts vii. 53; Heb. ii. 2.
20 the hand *m* of a mediator.   Now a mediator is not *a mediator* *m* Ex. xx. 19, 21, 22;
21 of one,[21] *n* but God is one.   *Is* the law then against the prom- Deut. v. 5, 22, 23, 27,
   ises of God?   God forbid:[22] *o* for if there had been a law given 31; John i. 17; Acts
   which could have given life,[23] verily righteousness should have vii. 38; I Tim. ii. 5.
22 been by the law.[24]   But *p* the Scripture hath concluded[25] *q* all[26] *n* Rom. iii. 29, 30.
   under sin, *r* that the promise by faith of[27] Jesus Christ might *o* Chap. ii. 21. Ver. 8.
23 be given to them that believe.   But before faith came, we were *p* Rom. iii. 9, 19, 23; xi. 32.
   q Rom. iv. 11, 12, 16.
   r Rom. iv. 11, 12, 16.

[1] Even a man's covenant when it hath been ratified   [2] no one annulleth
[3] and to his seed (*after the verb on account of the emphasis on seed*)
[4] Now this is what I (mean to) say   [5] *omit that*   [6] a
[7] ratified (*or,* established) beforehand by God unto Christ. *Some of the oldest MSS. omit the words* unto Christ   [8] came   [9] annul
[10] so as to make void the promise   [11] *omit* the   [12] hath freely given
[13] What then is (*the use of*) the law?
[14] superadded (*according to the better reading* προσετέθη)   [15] *insert* the
[16] shall have come   [17] hath been made   [18] *omit* and it was
[19] being ordained through   [20] by
[21] Now the (*the art. is generic*) mediator is not of one (*a mediator does not
   belong to one party, but requires at least two parties*)
[22] Far be it (*or,* May it never happen)   [23] such as could make alive
[24] would, indeed, have come from law   [25] shut up
[26] all things (τὰ πάντα)   [27] in

kept under the law, shut up [28] unto the faith which should after-
24 wards be revealed.[29]   Wherefore *the law was our schoolmaster
to bring us unto Christ,[30] 'that we might be justified by faith.
25   But after that faith is come, we are no longer under a school-
26 master.[31]   For "are all the children [32] of God by [33] faith, in
27 Christ Jesus.   For "as many of you as have been [34] baptized
28 "into Christ *have [35] put on Christ.   *There is neither Jew
   nor Greek, *there is neither bond nor free, *there is neither [36]
29 male nor [37] female : for ye are all [38] *one in Christ Jesus. And
   *if ye *be* [39] Christ's, then are ye Abraham's seed, and [40] *heirs
   according to the [41] promise.

[28] we were shut up and kept in ward under the law
[29] for the faith about to be revealed
[30] So then the law hath been our tutor unto Christ   [31] tutor
[32] sons   [33] through   [34] were   [35] did   [36] no   [37] and
[38] all are   [39] are   [40] *omit* and   [41] *omit* the

s Matt. v. 17;
Rom. x. 4;
Col. ii. 17;
Heb. ix. 9,
10.
t Acts xiii. 39;
chap. ij. 16.
u Chap. iv. 5,
6; John i.
12; Rom.
viii. 14, 15;
16; 1 John
iii. 1, 2.
v Rom. vi. 3.
w Matt.
xxviii. 19.
x Rom. xiii.
14.
y Chap. v. 6.
z Col. iii. 11.
a Comp. 1
Cor. xi. 11.
b John x. 16;
xvii. 20, 21
Eph. ii. 14,
15, 16; iv. 4,
15.
c Gen. xxi. 10,
12; Rom.
ix. 7; Heb.
xi. 18.
d Rom. viii.
17; chap.
iv. 7, 28; Eph. iii. 6.

Ver. 15. **Brethren.** Winning address, contrast-
ing with the severe rebuke, ver. 1 ; comp. iv. 31 ;
vi. 1. 'There is a touch of tenderness in the appeal here, as if to make amends for the severity
of the foregoing rebuke' (Lightfoot). — **After the
manner of men**, refers to the following illustration
taken from human relations. An argument *a
fortiori.* If even changeable men keep legal con-
tracts sacred, how much more the unchangeable
God. The Judaizers altered the covenant with
Abraham by adding new conditions, and thus virtually set it aside. — **Covenant.** Such was the
nature of the promise of God to Abraham (Gen.
xv. 18 ; xii. 7). The translation 'will,' 'testament' (in the margin of the E. V.), is unsuited to
the connection, and the translation 'promise' is
ungrammatical. In the Septuagint and in the
Greek Testament, the word διαθήκη always means
'covenant,' except in Heb. ix. 15-17, and the
rendering of the E. V. 'testament' (from the
Vulgate, and in accordance with classical usage)
in Matt. xxvi. 28, and other passages should be
corrected. The designation of the 'Old and New
Testament' (instead of 'Covenant') arose from
this mistranslation, and is especially improper in
the case of the Old Covenant (since God cannot
die), but has become so well established that it
must be retained.
Ver. 16 introduces the new idea that the covenant of promise was not made with Abraham
only, but with his whole seed which centres in
Christ, and was therefore still waiting its fulfilment at the time when the law was given; so that
it could not be abolished by the law. The emphasis lies on the words : 'and to his seed,'
which look beyond the law of Moses and to
Christ's coming. — **And to thy seed,** Gen. xiii. 15 ;
xvii. 8 : 'And I will give unto thee, and thy seed
after thee, the land wherein thou art a stranger,
all the land of Canaan, for an everlasting possession ; and I will be their God.' The promised inheritance refers evidently in its next and
literal sense to the land of Canaan, but in its
deeper spiritual sense to the kingdom of Christ.

The seed of Abraham comprehends, therefore,
not only the Israelites under Moses and Joshua,
but above all Christ and his people as the true
spiritual Israel who enter into that heavenly rest,
of which the rest of the earthly Canaan was only
an imperfect type (comp. Heb. iv. 8).
**He saith not, 'And to seeds' as of many, but
as of one, 'And to thy seed.'** There arises a difficulty here from the stress which Paul lays on
the singular of the word 'seed;' inasmuch as this
is a *collective* noun in Hebrew (*sera*) as well as in
the Greek (*sperma*), and modern languages, and
includes the whole posterity. It is singular in
form, but plural in meaning. The plural (*seraim,
spermata*) occurs in the sense of 'grains of wheat'
or 'grains of seed' (or *crop, produce* of the field,
1 Sam. viii. 15), but never in the sense of 'offspring' or 'posterity.' Hence it has been said
that Paul, after the 'manner of man' (ver. 15),
accommodates himself merely to the prevailing
rabbinical method of interpretation, or (as St.
Jerome thought) to the capacity of the 'foolish
Galatians.' Luther remarks : 'My dear brother
Paul, this argument won't stick.' But Paul under
stood Hebrew and Greek as well as his ancient
and modern interpreters, and he himself uses the
word *sperma*, 'offspring,' in the sense of plurality
(Rom. iv. 18 ; ix. 7), and the plural *spermata* in
the sense of 'various kinds of grain' (1 Cor. xv.
38). He reads it as it were between the lines of
the text. It is not a question of grammar, but of
spiritual meaning. The grammatical form (*sperma*
and *spermata*) serves merely as a vehicle of his
idea for the Greek reader. The main point is that
the *collective* word *seed* is used instead of *children*
or *descendants*, and that this word *seed* denotes
an organic unity of true spiritual Abrahamites,
and not all the carnal descendants of Abraham,
as the Jews imagined (comp. vers. 28, 29 ; Rom.
iv. 16, 18 ; ix. 8). The promise refers to Christ
par excellence, and to all those and *only* those
who are truly members of His body and united
to Him by a living faith. If all the single descendants of Abraham as such were meant, the

children of Hagar and Ketura, and subsequently Esau with his posterity would have to be included also; and yet they are plainly excluded. We must, therefore, look to the *believing* posterity, which is comprehended in Christ as the living head, the same Christ, in whom as the true seed of Abraham, God had promised to bless all the nations of the earth (Gen. xxii. 18; xxvi. 4; xviii. 14. — **Which is Christ,** *i. e.,* Christ, not as a single individual, but as the head of the church, which is 'His body, the fulness of Him who filleth all in all' (Eph. i. 23). In Him the whole spiritual race of Abraham is summed up, and in Him it fulfilled its mission to the whole world. He is the representative and embodiment of all true Israelites, and without Him the Jewish people has no meaning. The seed includes, therefore, all true believers who are vitally united to Christ. The key to the passage is in vers. 28 and 29: 'Ye are *all one* in Christ Jesus. And if ye be Christ's, then are ye Abraham's seed, heirs according to the promise.' Comp. 1 Cor. xii. 12: 'As the body is one and hath many members, and all the members of that one body, being many, are one body: so also is Christ.'

Ver. 17 contains an inference from ver. 15, in the form of a condensed restatement of the argument. It is impossible that the law should cancel the promise which was given repeatedly at least four hundred and thirty years earlier to the patriarchs, and which looked from the beginning to Christ as the proper end, so that the law is only an intervening link between the promise and its fulfilment. The words **unto** (with a view to) **Christ** (not *'in* Christ,' as in the E. V.), are, however, omitted in the oldest MSS. and critical editions. — **Now this I say.** What I mean to say is this. — **The law which came** (so long a time as) **four hundred and thirty years after** (the promise). This is the exact time of the sojourn of the Israelites in Egypt, according to the historical statement in Exod. xii. 40. In the prophetic passage (Gen. xv. 13. and in Acts vii. 6), the round number four hundred is given for this sojourn. The Hebrew text in both passages implies that the residence in Egypt only is meant. If Paul followed the Hebrew text, he did not include the patriarchal age from Abraham's immigration to Canaan till Jacob's emigration to Egypt, which would make about two hundred years more (630); the starting-point with him was the *close* of the patriarchal age, during which the promise was repeatedly given to Isaac and Jacob as well as to Abraham (hence the plural 'promises' in vers. 17 and 21). It is quite possible, however, that the Apostle follows here as often the text of the Septuagint which differs from the Hebrew in Ex. xii. 40, by including the patriarchal period in the four hundred and thirty years, and thus reducing the length of the Egyptian sojourn nearly one half: 'The sojourning of the children of Israel who dwelt in Egypt [*and in the land of Canaan*], was four hundred and thirty years.' The words 'and in the land of Canaan' are not in the Hebrew text, but are also found in the Samaritan Pentateuch. Josephus is inconsistent, and sometimes follows the one, sometimes the other chronology. The Septuagint may have inserted the explanatory clause to adapt the text to the chronological records of Egypt. But this difference in the chronology of the Greek Bible and our present Hebrew text, although very serious in a historical point of view, is of no account

for the argument in hand. Paul means to say, the older an agreement the stronger is its authority. The Hebrew text would strengthen the argument.

Ver. 18. If 'the inheritance,' *i. e.,* all the temporal and spiritual blessings promised to Abraham and culminating in the Christian salvation (comp. the word 'inheritance,' Matth. v. 5; Acts xx. 32; 1 Cor. vi. 9; Gal. v. 21), proceeded from the law and depended on its observance, it could be no more the gift of promise or of free grace, which can be apprehended only by a living faith. This, however, is plainly contradicted by the case of Abraham, who received the inheritance by free grace, and not by law, which then was not yet given. Law and works are inseparably connected, and so are promise (or grace) and faith. **Law** and **promise** are used here without the article as representing two opposite principles. — **Hath freely given,** bestowed it as a free gift. 'The perfect tense marks the permanence of the effect' (Lightfoot).

Ver. 19. **What then is the law?** Since the law has properly nothing to do with the Christian salvation, the question arises: To what end was it then given at all, what is its use and import? The difficulty leads the Apostle to a profound exposition of the relation of the Mosaic to the Christian religion. — **It was superadded because of the transgressions.** — It was not the original scheme, but a subsequent addition to the promise for an interimistic educational purpose to prepare the way for the fulfilment of the promise in Christ by the development of the disease of sin which is necessary to its cure. Comp. Rom. v. 20, 'the law came in beside,' etc. 'Because of,' or for the sake of, on account of. This is differently interpreted: (1.) In order to *restrain* or check transgressions; the law being a bridle to sin (a *Riegel* and *Zügel*) and preventing it from gross outbreaks (1 Tim. i. 9, 10). The Jews were, indeed, more moral in their outward deportment than the heathen. But this did not generally predispose them more favorably for the gospel. And then Paul speaks here not of the general restrictive and detective significance of the law which it has to this day, but simply of its propædeutic office as a preparation for Christ (comp. ver. 24 ff.). (2.) In order to *punish* the transgressor, and thus to quicken the moral sense and the desire for redemption. (3.) In order to *multiply* the transgressions ('for the benefit of,' comp. the Gr. χάριν here used); the law acting as a stimulant on the sinful desire, and calling it out into open exercise (Rom. v. 20; vii. 5, 7, 8, 10; 1 Cor. xv. 56). This bad effect arises not from the law itself, which is good and holy (Rom. vii. 12, 14, 22), and which was one of the great blessings of Israel (Rom. ix. 4), but from the sinful nature of man whose bad passions are pricked and roused by the law, so that the very prohibition tempts him to transgression (vii. 13 ff.; viii. 3). (4.) In order to bring sin to light, and to make it appear in its true character as a transgression of the divine law, and thus, by the knowledge of the disease, to prepare its cure. Comp. Rom. iv. 15: 'Where no law is, there is no transgression;' iii. 20: 'By the law is the knowledge of sin;' vii. 7, 8: 'Without the law sin was dead.' The choice lies between the last two interpretations, which are, in fact, closely connected; for it is by the very development of sin in the form of transgression that its true nature is understood, the sense of guilt awakened, and the desire for deliverance increased.

The disease of sin must reach the crisis before the restoration could take place, and so far we may say that God willed the development of sin with the view to its complete suppression by the future redemption. Comp. Rom. v. 20 : 'The law came in beside, that the trespass might abound ; but where sin abounded, the gift of grace did still more abound.' — **The seed,** *i. e.,* Christ, as in v. 16, — **Being ordained** (or **enacted**) by angels (by the ministry of angels). According to Josephus and the Jewish tradition, the angels acted as the ministers and organs of God in the promulgation of the Mosaic law. The angels mediated between God and Moses, and Moses mediated between the angels and the people of Israel. This view is based upon the Septuagint translation of Deut. xxxiii. 2 ('Jehovah .... shined forth from Mount Paran, and He came with ten thousands of *saints,*' to which the Septuagint adds : 'on his right hand *the angels* with him'), and indorsed in two other passages of the New Testament (Acts vii. 53, 58, and Heb. ii. 2. It may be inferred from the general mode of divine revelation which is mediated through agencies. — **Through the hand of a mediator,** *i. e.,* Moses, who received (on Mount Sinai) the tables of the law from God through the angels, and brought them down to the people. Hence he is often called *Mediator* in Rabbinical books. There were thus two intervening links between Jehovah and the people, a human mediator (Moses), and superhuman agents of God (the angels). This double agency may have been mentioned here either for the purpose of lowering the law in comparison with the gospel where God spoke in his Son directly to men and invites them to commune with Him without the mediation of man or angel ; or for the purpose of enhancing the solemnity of the enactment of the law as a preparation for the gospel. The view we take of this design, depends somewhat on the interpretation of ver. 20.

Most of the ancient fathers falsely refer the passage to Christ, misled by 1 Tim. ii. 5. But He is the mediator of the gospel, not of the law. Comp. Heb. viii. 6; ix. 15; xii. 24. Here he would be coördinated with, or rather subordinated to, the angels and represented as a mere agent, which is altogether foreign to the mind of Paul. Some modern interpreters think of the Metatron, the Angel of the Covenant, who according to the latter Jewish theology instructed Moses in the law. Ver. 20. The natural translation and meaning of this famous cross of interpreters seems to be this : Now a mediator (every mediator, including Moses, ver. 19)[1] is not of one (of one party only, but always presupposes two or more parties ; in this case God and the Jewish people) ; but God is one (either *one* numerically, i. e., *one* party, Israel being the other ; or *one* morally and emphatically, *i. e., one* only in opposition to every plurality or contradiction). But what is the bearing of this sentence upon the argument ? We have here evidently an elliptic syllogism, and must supply a link, either the minor proposition or the conclusion. The Apostle, as by an incidental stroke of lightning, suggests a collateral proof to the main idea of this section, namely, that the promise could not be made void by the law, in this sense : 'The God who gave both the promise and the law is *one* and the same, consistent in all his dealings, and cannot contradict himself, therefore the law cannot set aside the promise.' Or the Apostle suggests a proof for the inferiority of the law as compared with the promise, in this sense : 'The law is a covenant between two parties and is conditioned by the obedience of the people ; but the promise is the free gift of God alone, and man is merely the recipient ; the law may be broken by sinful men, the promise of God is unconditional and irrevocable.' These are the two most natural interpretations. I prefer the former because it falls in easier with the preceding verses 15-19.

Excursus on Chapter III. 20.

The genius of Paul, by the wealth and depth of his ideas, has stimulated more minds and exercised more pens than any other writer. This verse is counted the most difficult passage in the New Testament, and has given rise to about three hundred interpretations (254, according to Drs. Winer and Weigand in 1821 ; 430, according to Dr. Jowett.) Most of them are of recent origin, and not a few are more obscure than the text.[2]

The sentence is simple enough grammatically ; the obscurity arises from its brevity and connection. The interpretations differ (1) as to the sense of '*the mediator*' — whether it means all mediators as a class (the generic article), or Moses, or Christ ; (2) in what is to be supplied to the genitive *of one* (ἑνός) — party, thing, seed, people (the Jews only as distinct from the heathen, but God is the one God of both) ; (3) as to the meaning of 'God is *one* (εἷς) — numerically, or morally, referring to his monarchy, or sovereignty, or faithfulness and unchangeableness' ; (4) in the logical connection with the preceding and succeeding verses ; (5) in the relation of the clauses to each other.

Omitting mere arbitrary conjectures and fancies, we will give only the best interpretations.

1. *Christ* is the mediator between God and men. Comp. 1 Tim. ii. 5 : 'There is one God and one mediator between God and men, the man Christ Jesus.' — So most of the fathers who cared little for the logical connection, and hence did not feel the difficulty of the passage. Some saw here even a reference to the two natures of Christ, the human ('of one ') and the divine.

2. *Moses* is the mediator between God and the Jewish people ; but God is one, the same who gave the promise to Abraham and the law through Moses. — So Theodoret and other fathers. Bengel and

---

[1] The definite article in Greek is used here idiomatically in the generic sense, where the English idiom requires the indefinite article. Comp. "sin" and "death," as a power, in Rom. v. 12, where the Greek has the definite article (as also the German); also John x. 11 ; 2 Cor. xii. 12 (in Greek).
[2] The latest monograph is by Dr. Gust. Ad. Fricke, of Leipzig: *Das exegetische Problem im Briefe Pauli an die Galater. c. iii. 20,* Leipzig, 1880, 52 pages. The older monographs are mentioned by Winer, De Wette, Meyer, and Wieseler

Wieseler also refer ' the mediator ' to Moses, but differ in the conclusion. Wieseler supplies the inference : the failure of the mediatorial office of Moses between God and the people is due to the unfaithfulness of *men* who did not keep the compact.

3. A mediator (generally) is not of one party, but of two ; God is one party, the people the other ; and the people are bound to observe the law. The last sentence is supplied. — So Winer, who sees here a parenthetical remark in favor of the authority of the law.

4. A mediator occupies a subordinate middle position and belongs to both parties who stand over against each other ; but God is one party for himself over and above the mediator. The law belongs to the same subordinate sphere as the mediator, but the promise which is given directly by God without a mediator, stands higher. The law was provisional, the promise is permanent. — So Baur, followed by Farrar (*St. Paul*, ii. 150).

5. A mediator implies a separation of two parties, God and man, but in God, the author of the promise, is perfect unity. An argument for the superiority of the promise. — De Wette.

6. Every mediator intervenes between two or more parties ; but God is a single person, not a plurality ; hence the law, which is a contract between God and Israel, cannot be opposed to the divine promises of the same one God acting directly. — Meyer.

7. The idea of a mediator supposes two different parties to be united ; but inasmuch as God is strictly *one* — so that there can be no two Gods, or one God of the law and another of the promise — it follows that Moses as mediator did not mediate between the God of the promise and the God of the law and so abolish the promise by the law, but he mediated (as is well known) only between God and the people of Israel. — Ewald. Similarly Weiss (*Bibl. Theol. d. N. T.*, 3d ed., p. 266).

8. God in the promise stands and acts alone ; therefore in the promise a mediator does not appertain to God. Is then the law which involved a mediator opposed to the promises which rested on God alone ? God forbid. — Ellicott.

9. The sentence is an attack upon the law and the Judaizers. A mediator, and consequently also the law which was given by mediators (angels and Moses), does not appertain to the promise which proceeds from God alone. — Holsten (in the *Protestanten-Bibel*, 1874). — Similarly Fricke : Moses and the law belong to the sphere of mediation between two parties at least ; the promises were given by God *alone* to Abraham (ver. 16) ; consequently the law and the promise do not agree, and cannot be reconciled except in the way pointed out, vers. 21–24.

10. The very idea of mediation supposes a contract to which there are at least two parties. But where there is a contract there must be also conditions, and if these conditions are not observed the whole falls to the ground. The law was such a contingent contract, and as it was not kept, the blessings annexed to it were forfeited. On the other hand, the promise is absolute and unconditioned, it depends upon God alone. He gave it freely, and He will assuredly keep it, no matter what man may do. God alone is concerned in it. — This is substantially the interpretation of Schleiermacher, Usteri, Reuss, Lightfoot, Sanday. Reuss (in his French *Commentary*) thus clearly puts it : ' A mediator implies two contracting parties, consequently two wills, which may be united, but may also disagree ; a law therefore given by mediation is conditional and imperfect ; but the promise, emanating from God *alone* and having His will for its sole source and guarantee, is infinitely more sure and more elevated. The law, then, cannot set aside the promise, its aim can only be secondary.'

Ver. 21. If the law had the power to break sin and to impart righteousness and life, it would indeed be a rival of the promise and enter into conflict with it. But this is not the aim of the law at all ; on the contrary it is intended merely to bring sin to its proper crisis and thereby to prepare the fulfilment of the promise. Paul infers from the effect of the law its proper character and relation to the promise. **Make alive** implies that we are spiritually dead by nature. — **Indeed**, truly, in reality. But Paul maintains, in opposition to the vain conceit of the self-righteous Jews and Judaizing Christians, that the law condemns all alike.

Ver. 22. **The Scripture**, the whole Old Testament, including the law. It is here personified as in ver. 8, and stands for the author of the Scripture. The Apostle may have had in mind a special passage, as Ps. cxliii. 2 (quoted above ii. 16) or Deut. xxvii. 26 (quoted iii. 10), or rather the general scheme of the Scripture as a history of the fall and redemption. **Shut up all (things) under sin.** Comp. Rom. xi. 32 : ' God shut up all (men) in unbelief (or disobedience), that He might have mercy upon all.' These two passages contain, as in a nutshell, the whole history of men, the mystery of the fall cleared up by the greater mystery of redemption. ' Shut up,' as in a prison and state of complete slavery, without means of escape, in striking contrast with the freedom of the gospel. The verb implies an effective (not simply a declaratory) activity of God in the development and punishment (not in the origin) of sin, and this activity is conditioned and controlled by the eternal counsel of redeeming love. ' All ' things, the most comprehensive term. In the parallel passage, Rom. xi. 32, the masculine is used, 'all' men. They are viewed as one solid mass of corruption and guilt. No exception is made, not even in favor of the Virgin Mary, as the Vatican dogma would require. The second clause, **that** (in order that, with the intention that) **the promise**, etc., contains the solution of the problem in the first clause. God wills sin only as something to be overcome and destroyed ; He permitted the fall of Adam only in view of the redemption by Christ which more than made up for all the loss of the fall.

' In Christ the tribes of Adam boast
More blessings than their father lost.'—(*Watts.*)

' Earth has a joy unknown in heaven
The new-born peace of sin forgiven.
Tears of such pure and deep delight,
Ye angels ! never dimmed your sight.'
(*A. L. Hillhouse.*)

Ver. 23. **Before the faith came,** the faith in Jesus Christ just mentioned (ver. 22), which under the legal dispensation existed only as a latent element of life. — **We were shut up and kept in ward under the law for the faith about to be revealed,** *i. e.,* in order to be prepared for the free state of the Christian faith. The word 'faith' usually means the *subjective* state of the heart, the exercise of trust; but in vers. 22 and 23 it seems to pass over into the *objective* sense, *i. e.,* the dispensation of faith, the gospel, hence the verbs *came* and *to be revealed.* In ver. 24 again the subjective sense is meant.

Ver. 24. **So then the law has been our tutor unto Christ.** This sentence expresses in a few words the true philosophy of the law in its relation to Christ. — 'Tutor,' literally *pædagogue* (leader of boys), one intrusted with the moral supervision and instruction of minors. In Greek and Roman families of rank the office of tutor was intrusted to a reliable slave who had to watch the children of his master in their plays, to keep them from excess and folly, to lead them to school, or instruct them himself in the elementary branches, and thus to train them for the freedom of youth and manhood. This pædagogic mission attaches not only to the law of Moses, but we may say to all laws, also to the moral law of nature written in the conscience of man. The discipline of law and authority is still the school of moral freedom, and reaches its proper end in self-government which is true freedom. The Greek fathers called philosophy the pædagogue of the Gentiles, which prepared them theoretically for Christianity, as the Mosaic law prepared the Jews practically. — The 'schoolmaster' of the E. V. expresses only one element in the office of the law. Luther's version: *Zuchtmeister,* is better, because more comprehensive. It is still wider of the mark and inconsistent with the imagery of the context to make Christ the schoolmaster ('the tutor to conduct us to the school of Christ'). On the contrary the whole work of preparatory training belongs to the pædagogue, and Christ represents here the result of the educational process, *i. e.,* the state of evangelical freedom and independent, self-governing manhood. Comp. Eph. iv. 13.

Ver. 26. **For ye all are sons of God.** 'All,' Jews and Gentiles alike (comp. vers. 27 and 28). 'Sons' (not 'children,' E. V.), implies here the idea of age and freedom, as distinct from the state of childhood and pupilage under the training of the pædagogue. Comp. iv. 6, 7; Rom. viii. 14, 15. Paul uses the term 'sons' and 'children' of God mostly in opposition to slaves (Gal. iv. 7). John uses the term 'children' of God with reference to their new birth (John i. 12; 1 John iii. 1, 2, 10; v. 2) — **By the faith,** which is the act of a freeman, **in Christ Jesus** (the dative in Greek) *i. e.,* reposing in Christ, or (if we prefer connecting the words with 'sons') by virtue of your life-union with Christ, being grounded and rooted in Him.

Ver. 27. **As many of you as were baptized into Christ, did put on Christ.** The Greek tenses (aorists) make the two acts simultaneous; in the act and at time of your baptism ye did clothe yourselves with Christ. 'Into' implies introduction into union with Christ, mystical incorporation in Christ; so also Rom. vi. 3 ('into Christ'; comp. 1 Cor. x. 2 'into Moses'), and the baptismal formula, Matt. xxviii. 19, 'baptizing into (not 'in') the name of the Father, and the Son, and

the Holy Ghost.' — 'Did put on Christ,' is analogous to the phrase 'to put on the new man' of righteousness and holiness, in opposition to the 'old man' of sin which is to be 'put away;' Eph. iv. 22, 24; Col. iii. 9, 10. The baptized is surrounded by Christ and covered with his merits, as the soldier is surrounded by his equipment. This is, however, only the beginning of the Christian life and must be followed by daily renewal and progress. Comp. Rom. xiii. 14. The figure of putting on Christ as a new dress gave rise afterwards to the custom of wearing white baptismal garments, but there is no trace that such a custom existed already in the Apostolic church.

To understand this passage, we should remember that in the Apostolic age the baptism of adults (such as are here addressed) presupposed or implied, as a rule, actual conversion and regeneration in consequence of preaching and instruction, though there were exceptions (as the case of Simon Magus, who hypocritically confessed faith). If baptism of believers on personal profession of faith means anything, it means the death of the old man of sin and the birth of the new man of righteousness. This is its idea and aim, but practically it may be and often is profaned and perverted. On the part of God it is a sign and seal of remission of sin and of regeneration by the Holy Spirit, on the part of man an act of self-consecration to the service of God (comp. Rom. vi. 3, 4; Tit. iii. 5). From this high estimate Paul derives the strongest exhortations to the baptized, to walk in accordance with their solemn pledge, lest by their own faithlessness they forfeit the baptismal blessing. The greater the benefit, the greater the responsibility and risk. Here he represents the putting on of Christ as a finished fact (in principle), elsewhere he urges it upon those already baptized as a daily duty (Rom. xiii. 14). The former is the dogmatic, the latter the ethical view of the matter. Calvin remarks that sacraments are never meant to be empty signs, but include always, according to the divine will, the thing signified. The believer receives the grace offered, the unbeliever rejects it, but he cannot by such rejection overthrow the faithfulness of God, nor deprive the sacraments of their true objective intent and significance. Thus the sun shines upon the blind as well as the seeing, but although the blind man has no benefit from the sun, he cannot alter the nature of the sun, or deprive him of his force. Food is always nourishing and salutary in itself, though it may prove poison to the sick.

Ver. 28. **There is neither Jew nor Greek,** etc., there is no room for, and there can be no room. Paul negatives, 'not the fact only, but the possibility, as James i. 17.' The great idea of freedom, fraternity, and equality, then, is to be traced to Christianity, although it is often carnally misunderstood and caricatured by men. Error steals the livery of truth, and anti-Christ the livery of Christ. It is to be understood here, of course, in a religious sense. The gospel makes all men equal before God, both as sinners, and as subjects of redeeming grace; it has broken down the national, social, and sexual partition walls of the ancient world, and raised women and slaves to the true dignity and the enjoyment of the rights of man, not in the violent way of a sudden revolution, but by the slow and silent, yet sure process of a moral transformation of society from within, a process still going on till its final consummation at the second coming of Christ. — For ye all are one (man) in Christ Jesus, one moral person in Jesus Christ the head, comp. Eph. ii. 15 ('one new man'); 1 Cor. xii. 12. The masculine gender in the original is chosen on account of ver. 16, and is more expressive in this connection than the neuter, which we find in John x. 30; xvii. 11, 21.

Ver. 29. And if ye are Christ's, then are ye Abraham's seed, heirs according to promise. The final conclusion of this profound, comprehensive, varied, and terse reasoning, in proof of the assertion ver. 7, that the believers are the true children of Abraham, and consequently heirs by promise. Ver. 16 must here be kept in view, where Christ is declared to be the seed of Abraham. Union with Christ constitutes the true spiritual descent from Abraham, and secures the inheritance of all the Messianic blessings by promise, as against inheritance by law.

CHAPTER IV.

I. Continuation: The State of Adoption contrasted with the State of Legal Slavery under the Law, vers. 1-11; II. Affectionate Appeal to the Galatians by further calling to Remembrance their former Personal Attachment to Paul, vers. 12-20; III. Continuation of the Argument by a Biblical Allegory, vers. 21-31

The State of Adoption contrasted with the State of Slavery under the Law.

Chapter IV. 1-11.

The Apostle proceeds to give a fuller exposition of the divine sonship and heirship, ch. iii. 29, and shows that the believers under the old dispensation, though sons and heirs in principle and prospect, were yet actually in a state of pupilage, and hence had no more freedom than a slave; while now with the coming of Christ the time of majority has arrived. Then he gives utterance to his painful surprise at the relapse of the Galatians to their former state of pupilage and slavery.

1 NOW[1] I say, *That* the heir, as long as he is a child,[2] differeth nothing from a servant,[3] though he be[4] lord of all;
2 But is under tutors,[5] and governors[6] until the time appointed[7]
3 of[8] the father. Even so we,[9] when we were children,[10] *a* were in
4 bondage[11] under the elements of the world: But *b* when the fulness of the time was come,[12] God sent forth his Son, *c* made[13]
5 *d* of a woman, *e* made under the law, *f* To redeem them that were under the law, *g* that we might receive the adoption of sons.[14]
6 And because ye are sons, God hath[15] sent forth *h* the Spirit of
7 his Son into your[16] hearts, crying, Abba, Father. Wherefore thou art no more a servant,[17] but a son; *i* and if a son, then an heir of God through Christ.[18]
8 Howbeit then,[19] *k* when ye knew not God, *l* ye did service[20] unto
9 them which by nature are no gods.[21] But now, *m* after that ye have known God, or rather are known of God,[22] *n* how turn ye

a Vers. 8, 9; chap. ii. 4; v. 1; Col. ii. 8, 20; Heb. ix. 10.
b Gen. xlix. 10; Dan. ix. 24; Mark i. 15; Eph. i. 10.
c John i. 14; Rom. i. 3; Phil. ii. 7; Heb. ii. 14.
d Gen. iii. 15; Is. vii. 14; Mic. v. 3; Matt. i. 23; Luke i. 31; ii. 7.
e Matt. v. 17; Luke ii. 27.
f Matt. xx. 28; chap. iii. 13; Eph. i. 7; Tit. ii. 14; Heb. ix. 12; 1 Peter i. 18, 19.
g John i. 12; chap. iii. 26; Eph. i. 5.
h Rom. v. 5; viii. 15.
i Rom. viii. 16, 17; iii. 29.
k Eph. ii. 12; 1 Thess. iv. 5.
l Rom. i. 25; 1 Cor. viii. Eph. ii. 11, 12; 1 Thess. i. 9.
m 1 Cor. viii. 3; xiii. 12; 2 Tim. ii. 19.
n Chap. iii. 3; Col. ii. 20.

---

[1] But   [2] that so long as the heir is an infant (minor) he
[3] slave (*or* bondman)   [4] is   [5] guardians   [6] stewards
[7] the day pre-appointed   [8] by   [9] So we also
[10] infants (minors)   [11] were enslaved   [12] came   [13] born
[14] the sonship (*or* adoption into sonship)   [15] *omit* hath   [16] our
[17] no longer a slave (*or* bondman)
[18] an heir through God (*omit* through Christ)   [19] But formerly
[20] ye were in bondage   [21] to those who by nature are not gods
[22] but now having come to know God, or rather being known of God

again to [9] the weak and beggarly elements, whereunto [23] ye de- ^{[9] Rom. viii. 3; Heb. vii. 18}
10 sire again [24] to be in bondage ? [p] Ye observe [25] days, and ^{Rom. xiv. 5; Col. ii. 16.}
11 months, and times,[26] and years.   I am afraid of you, [q] lest I ^{[q] Chap. ii. 2 · v. 2, 4; 1 Thess. iii. 5.}
have bestowed upon you labour [27] in vain.

[23] to which   [24] over again   [25] Or, Do ye (scrupulously) observe . . . ?
[26] seasons   [27] lest haply I have toiled for you.

Ver. 1. **But what I would say is this, that so long as the heir is an infant (a minor), he differeth nothing from a slave, though he is lord of all**, owner of the whole patrimony or inheritance by right and prospectively, but not in actual possession. In human relations the taking possession of the inheritance is conditioned by the death of the parent, or at all events by a corresponding loss ; while God gives to his children at the appointed time all the blessings of salvation without losing anything, since He is the living fountain and preserver of all. But in both cases the majority of the heir is presupposed. The heir in his nonage represents the Jewish people and the state of the world before Christ.

Ver. 2. **Under guardians** (including the tutor or pedagogue) **and stewards**, who control the person and the property of the minor till he becomes of age, which the Hebrew law fixed at thirteen years and one day, the Roman law at the twenty-fifth year. — **Until the day pre-appointed**, or day fixed beforehand. A legal term (one word in Greek, *prothesmia*) signifying the time allowed to elapse before bringing an action, the time fixed by the statute of limitations (*Tag der Verjährung*); then any pre-appointed time or day ; here the time when the office of the guardian terminates. — **By the father.** Among the Hebrews, Greeks, and Romans, the period of pupilage or nonage was fixed by law, and not dependent upon the arbitrary will of the parent. But this makes no difference in the argument, the divine will being the fountain of all law, and having foreordained from eternity the time of Christ's coming. Paul speaks ' theologically rather than juridically.' It is not necessary therefore to suppose that he referred to the Keltic custom, which gave the father a more unlimited power over his children.

Ver. 3. **So we also, when we were minors,** the Jewish Christians before their conversion, comp. iii. 23. In a wider sense the words are applicable to the heathen Christians also, whose former religion was still more childish, though not divinely appointed as a preparatory school. — **Enslaved under the elements** (or rudiments) **of the world.** Comp. ver. 9. This is understood by the church fathers in a physical, by most modern interpreters in an ethical sense.

(1.) The elementary substances of the external world or physical universe (so 2 Pet. iii. 10, 12), as earth, fire, and especially the heavenly bodies. (*a*) The Jewish festivals (sabbaths, new moons, and passovers) which were regulated by the course of the sun and moon, and so far by the powers of nature. (Chrysostom.) (*b*) The heathen worship of the stars and other material substances. (Augustine.) (*c*) Religion of earthly, sensuous forms and rites generally (both Jewish and heathen), as distinct from spiritual religion and rational worship. (Neander.) Against this interpretation in all its forms is the omission of *world* after *elements* in ver. 9.

(2.) The elementary lessons, rudimentary instruction, the alphabet of learning (as Hebr. v. 12 ; comp. Col. ii. 8, 20). So Jerome, Calvin, Olshausen, Meyer, Wieseler, Ellicott, Lightfoot. This is much simpler and better suited to the context. Paul represents here the religion before Christ, especially the Jewish, as an elementary religion or a religion of childhood, full of external rites and ceremonies, all of which had a certain educational significance, but pointed beyond themselves to an age of manhood in Christ. This falls in naturally with what he said in the preceding chapter of the pedagogical mission of the law. The whole Old Testament dispensation was an elementary or preparatory school for the gospel, a religion of types and shadows, of hope and promise, destined to lose itself in Christianity, as its substance and fulfilment. — **Of the world**, not the physical universe (as in the first interpretation of the ' elements '), but mankind which needed such a training for Christianity. The expression seems to imply that Paul comprehends the heathen also, comp. ver. 8. But the Jews were in fact the religious representatives of the whole race in its *motion towards Christ.*

Ver. 4. **When the fulness of the time came**, *i. e.,* when the period appointed by the Father (ver. 2) till the coming of Christ and the age of manhood was filled up or completed. This period was fixed in the eternal counsel of God with reference to the development of the race. The words ' fulness of the time ' express, as in a nutshell, the whole philosophy of history before Christ, and the central position of the incarnation. The ancient history of Jews and Gentiles was a preparation either direct or indirect, positive or negative, divine or human, for the coming of Christ, and Christ is the turning point of history, the end of the old, and the beginning of a new world. Hence we begin our era with His birth. He himself commenced his preaching with the declaration, Mark i. 15 : ' The time is fulfilled, and the kingdom of God is at hand.' The Saviour could not appear in any other country, nor at any other time, either sooner or later, nor in any other nation, according to the order of divine government and the preordained harmony of history. — **Sent forth his Son**, who, therefore, must have existed before the incarnation in heavenly glory with the Father. Comp. Col i. 15-19 ; John i. 1. — **Born of a woman**, is no allusion to the mystery of the supernatural conception (= ' of a virgin '), but expresses simply the realness of the incarnation or Christ's true humanity. Comp. Job xiv. 1, ' man that is born of a woman ; ' and Matt. xi. 11, ' among them that are born of women.' Every reader knew, of course, who the woman was. The absence of any further allusion to Mary in the Epistles of Paul, who never even mentions her name, goes to show that the excessive veneration of the holy Virgin, as it obtains in the Greek and Roman churches, arose after the Apostolic age. We meet it first in the apocryphal Gospels and then among the fathers of the fourth or fifth centuries, when the term 'mother of God' came into general use. — **Born under the law** (the accus. in Gr. implies the motion or transition from the preëxistent state into the state of human subjection to the law) is more specific, and defines the humanity of Christ as to its national and religious aspect. He was not only born of a woman, *i. e.*, a true man, like all others, but a full member of a particular nation and the Jewish theocracy, and hence subject to all its religious ordinances and obligations, in order to redeem those who were under the legal covenant. A Gentile could not have saved the world from the curse of the law; in Israel alone all the historical conditions were at hand; and hence, 'salvation is of the Jews' (John iv. 22), that from them it might pass over in proper order to the whole race.

Ver. 5 **To redeem,** to buy off from the curse and the slavery of the law. This he did by His perfect obedience and the bestowal of the spirit of love and freedom. — **Receive,** not *recover,* for the redemption by Christ infinitely transcends the original child-like innocence lost by Adam. — **The sonship,** through and for the sake of Jesus, the only begotten Son. He is the Son by nature and from eternity, we become sons by grace in time. The word 'sonship' or adoption as sons is used only by Paul, in five passages, Rom. viii. 15, 23; ix. 4; Eph. i. 5; while the term 'children of God' is more frequent. The former suits here better, as contrasted with slavery, and in distinction also from a state of mere pupilage. Both terms, 'sons' and 'children' of God, and the corresponding 'Father' never refer in the New Testament to the natural relation of man as the creature to God as the creator, but always to the moral and spiritual relation, which results from the new birth and the communication of the Holy Spirit.

Ver. 6. **God sent forth the Spirit of his Son into our hearts.** Comp. Rom. viii. 9, 14-17. The gift of the Spirit seems here to succeed the act of adoption, while in Rom. viii. 14-16 it is made to precede it. But there is between both an inseparable connection and mutual dependence, and the communication of the Spirit is not confined to a single act, but goes on increasing with the spiritual growth of the children of God. — 'Our' is better supported than 'your.' A similar change of person as in the preceding verse, resulting from the vivacity of speech and the sympathy with the reader. — **Crying ;** praying with strong desire and glowing fervor. Comp. Isa. xix. 20; James v. 4. In Rom. viii. 15, we read: 'in whom *we* cry.' Here the Spirit himself appears as praying, and the believer as the organ. The Holy Spirit so deeply sinks into the spirit of believers and so closely identifies himself with them that He prays in them and through them as their advocate. Christ is their advocate at the right hand of God, the Spirit is the 'other advocate' (E. V. 'comforter'), indwelling in their hearts. — **Abba, Father.** 'Abba' is the Aramaic word for 'Father' (in Hebrew *Aph*), so childlike in its very sound, and sanctioned by the beginning of the Lord's Prayer, as originally uttered, also by His prayer in Gethsemane, Mark xiv. 36. Hence Paul retains it here as in Rom. viii. 15. 'Father.' The

emphasizing combination of the familiar Hebrew with the corresponding Greek name was probably a liturgical formula among Hellenistic Jews and Christians. (Meyer regards 'Abba,' here as a proper name, which became the customary address to God in prayer after the example set by our Lord. Augustine and many others see here more than a translation, namely an allusion to the unity of the God of the Jews and of the Gentiles, and the unity of the Spirit, dwelling and praying in both.)

Ver. 7. **So that thou art no longer a slave, but a son,** etc. Inference from vers. 5 and 6. The second person individualizes and brings it home to each reader. — 'Son,' in opposition to 'slave,' but not, of course, to the exclusion of daughter. For the Apostle had distinctly declared, iii. 28, that the sexual, as well as other differences, disappear before Christ in the general religious equality. He had here in view probably not the Jewish, but the Roman law, which was most familiar to his readers and which gave daughters and sons, adopted as well as native children, a title to the inheritance; while the Jewish law excluded the daughters, except in default of male heirs (Num. xxvii. 1 ff.; xxxvi. 1 ff.), but required the first born son to support them till they were married. — **And if a son, then an heir through God.** This is the most approved reading, of which the received text: 'of God through Christ,' is a correct explanation, in conformity with Rom. viii. 17. The word 'God' is here used in the widest sense of the triune God, from whom we derive our sonship and heirship in opposition to the law and to carnal descent from Abraham. For the Father sends His only begotten Son, the Son delivers us from the slavery of the law and reconciles us to the Father, the Holy Spirit applies the sonship to our heart and bears witness to it.

Ver. 8. Here the Apostle evidently addresses Gentile Christians. But some may have been before their conversion proselytes to Judaism. — **But formerly** (before your conversion, comp. ver. 7) **when ye knew not God.** A description of the heathen state, which, compared with the knowledge of the only true and living God through revelation, was dark ignorance. Indefinite knowledge is definite ignorance. Comp. 1 Thess. iv. 5; 2 Thess. i. 8; Eph. ii. 12. Paul admits, however, Rom. i. 21, that the heathen have or might have an inferior order of knowledge from the light of nature (Rom. i. 21) and a moral sense of right and wrong (Rom. ii. 14-16), and are therefore without excuse. — **Ye were in bondage to those who by nature are not gods.**[1] This reading which connects the negative ('not') with 'gods,' and not with 'nature,' is best supported. It means that the heathen idols are not gods, but something else, namely, demons or evil spirits. Comp. 1 Cor. x. 20: 'the things which the Gentiles sacrifice, they sacrifice to *demons,* and not to God.' Accordingly the heathen divinities had a real existence, and idolatry was the religion of the devil and his army of fallen angels or evil spirits. Comp. also Deut. xxxii. 17; Ps. cvi. 37. If the negation is put before 'nature': 'to those who are gods not by nature,' we must supply: 'but only in repute' (comp. 1 Cor. viii. 5: 'though

---

[1] The oldest MSS. read τοῖς φύσει μὴ οὖσιν θεοῖς (supply, ἀλλὰ δαιμονίοις), the received text: τοῖς μὴ φύσει (supply ἀλλὰ λόγῳ, comp. 1 Cor. viii. 5, εἰσὶν λεγόμενοι θεοί) οὖσιν θεοῖς. In either case μή is a subjective negation and expresses the opinion of the writer.

there be that are *called* gods '). In this case the Apostle would deny the existence of the heathen gods altogether and hold them to be mere creatures of fancy (or personifications of the powers of nature).

Ver. 9. But now having come to know (or, to discern, to recognize) **God, or rather being known of God,** recognized and adopted as His own, as His children ; comp. 1 Cor. viii. 2. Formerly the Galatians were left to themselves and, as it were, ignored by God. Then their knowledge of God was not their own merit, but a free gift of God, who condescended to dwell in them and to enlighten their minds and hearts. Man's knowledge of God is very imperfect and has no value except as far as it flows from God's perfect knowledge and recognition of man. — **How is it that ye are turning back again to the weak and beggarly elements.** The term ' elements,' or ' rudiments ' embraces here both the heathen and the Jewish religion. Even Judaism is merely a poor elementary school and a system of slavery, as compared with the riches and freedom of the gospel. If we deprive Judaism of its Messianic features and divest the ritual law of its typical reference to Christ, it sinks virtually to the same level with the false religions. The relapse of the Galatians to such an unspiritual Judaism was therefore at the same time a relapse to their original heathenism. Hence the words ' again ' and ' once more.'

Ver. 10. Do ye (scrupulously) observe days, and months, and seasons, and years ? The interrogative form gives more vicacity to the passage and more weight to ver. 11. If it is not a question, it must be taken as an exclamation of painful surprise : ' Is it possible that you should observe !' The Apostle means a Judaistic, slavish, and superstitious observance which ascribes an intrinsic holiness to particular days and seasons (as if the other days and seasons were in themselves profane), and which makes such observance a necessary condition of justification (as if faith in Christ were not sufficient for justification). Such observance virtually derives salvation in some sense from the elements of nature, like the sun and the moon, which regulate the festival seasons. The polemic of Paul is equally applicable to a Judaizing, that is, slavish, superstitious, and self-righteous observance of Sunday or any other Christian festival. But there is also a free, evangelical, and spiritual observance of holy days and seasons, which is essential to proper order in social worship, and which the Apostle was far from condemning, since he himself distinguished in some way ' the first day ' of the week in commemoration of the resurrection (Acts xx. 7 ; 1 Cor. xvi. 2), and also the Passover and Pentecostal

seasons (Acts xviii. 21 ; xx. 6, 16; 1 Cor. v. 7, 8). —' Days,' the weekly sabbaths, and other single holy days and fast days. Some English commentators would exclude the weekly Sabbath, since it is enjoined in the Decalogue ; but this is arbitrary and contrary to the parallel passage, Col. ii. 16 ('sabbath days'). Paul denounces the Pharisaic sabbatarianism, as Christ Himself had done by word and example. It was a pedantic, mechanical, slavish observance which worshipped the letter and killed the spirit. Even Rabbi Gamaliel, Paul's teacher, and one of the most liberal of the Pharisees, was unwilling to unload his ass laden with honey on a sabbath day, and let the poor animal die. This was considered a proof of great piety. But it is a serious error to infer from this passage (and Col. ii. 16; Rom. xiv. 5) that the Sabbath is abolished in the Christian dispensation. The law of the Sabbath, *i. e.,* of one weekly day of holy rest in God (the seventh in the Jewish, the first in the Christian Church) is as old as the creation, it is founded in the moral and physical constitution of man, it was instituted in Paradise, incorporated in the Decalogue on Mount Sinai, put on a new foundation by the resurrection of Christ, and is an absolute necessity for public worship and the welfare of man. ' The Sabbath is made for man,' that is, instituted by God for man's spiritual and temporal benefit. So marriage is made for man, government is made for man. But the Judaizers reversed the order and made the Sabbath an end instead of a means, and a burden instead of a blessing. — ' Months,' the new moons (comp. Col. ii. 16), which were kept as joyful festivals by the Jews (Num. xxviii. 11-15), especially those of the seventh month, which had the same sacredness among the months of the year as the sabbath among the days of the week. — ' Seasons,' the festival seasons, which lasted several days, as the Passover, Pentecost, and the Feast of Tabernacles (Lev. xxiii. 4). — ' Years,' sabbatical (*i. e.,* every seventh) and jubilee (every fiftieth) years (Lev. xxv. 2-17). This does not necessarily imply that the Galatians were then actually celebrating a sabbatical year according to the Mosaic ritual ; the plural speaks against such a supposition. But this point belonged to their theory, which consistently must have led them to a corresponding practice as soon as the occasion presented itself.

Ver. 11. I am apprehensive of you, lest haply I have toiled for you in vain. This verse is, as it were, bathed in tears, and betrays the deep and painful solicitude of a faithful pastor for his stray sheep, or a tender father for his erring children. It leads to the affectionate appeal, ver. 12 ff.

---

2. *Affectionate Appeal to the Galatians.*

CHAPTER IV. 12-20.

Paul interrupts his argument for a moment by an affectionate appeal to the feelings of the Galatians. He reminds them of their former enthusiastic love and veneration for him, and seeks thus to regain their confidence. He wishes to force a passage through their heart to their conviction. To work upon the feelings is perfectly legitimate, and one of the most fruitful agencies of persuasion and conversion, but it must always be made subservient to the interests of truth.

12 BRETHREN, I beseech you, be as I *am* ; for I *am* as ye
13 are : [1] *a* ye have not injured me at all.[2]   Ye [3] know how *a* 2 Cor. ii. 5.
 b through infirmity [4] of the flesh I preached the gospel unto *b* 1 Cor. ii. 3 ;
                                                                     2 Cor. xi.
14 you *c* at the first.[5]   And my temptation [6] which was [7] in my *c* 30, xii. 7, 9.
                                                                            Chap. i. 6.
 flesh ye despised not, nor rejected ; [8] but [9] received me *d* as an *d* 2 Sam. xix.
                                                                           27 ; See
15 angel of God, *e even* as Christ Jesus.   Where is then the bless- Zech. xii. 8 ;
                                                                        Mal. ii. 7.
 edness ye spake of ? [10] for I bear you record,[11] that, if *it had e* Matt. x. 40 ;
                                                                       Luke x. 16 ;
 been [12] possible, ye would have plucked out your own eyes,[13] John xiii.
                                                                  20 ; 1 Thess.
16 and have [14] given them to me.   Am I therefore become your en- ii. 13.
17 emy, *f* because I tell [15] you the truth ?   They *g* zealously affect 16 *f* Chap. ii. 5,
                                                                             14.
 you, *but* not well ; yea, they would [17] exclude you, that ye might *g* Rom. x. 2 ;
                                                                        2 Cor. xi. 2.
18 affect [16] them.   But *it is* good to be zealously affected [18] always
 in *a* good *thing*,[19] and not only when I am present with you.
19 *h* My little children, of whom I travail in birth again [20] until *h* 1 Cor. iv. 15 ;
                                                                        Philem. 10 ;
20 Christ be formed in you, I desire [21] to be present with you now, James i. 18.
 and to change my voice ; for I stand in doubt of you.[22]

[1] Become as I, for I also *became* as you, brethren, I beseech you.
[2] Ye did me no injury ;   [3] ; but ye
[4] that on account of an infirmity   [5] the former time
[6] your trial   [7] *omit* which was   [8] ye did not scorn nor loathe
[9] ye   [10] your self-congratulation   [11] witness
[12] *omit, it had been*   [13] your eyes   [14] *omit* have
[15] enemy by telling   [16] court   [17] desire to
[18] courted   [19] *cause*   [20] I am again in travail
[21] but I could wish   [22] I am perplexed about you

Ver. 12. **Become as I** (am), **for I also** (became)
as you (are). Paul asks the Galatians to imitate
his example, that is, to cast off their Judaizing
tendency and to become simple, decided, and consistent Christians, as he had done himself when he
cast off his former Judaism, and when he placed
himself on a level with them in their heathen state
in order to win them to Christ.   I abandoned all
for you ; do the same for me.   Comp. ii. 14 ; 1
Cor. ix. 20, 21.   Others take the words to be an
exhortation to love him as he loved them, or to
enter as fully into his heart and sympathy, as he
had by love identified himself with them.   But
this does not fall in with the connection, and Paul
makes no complaint of a want of love to him. —
Brethren, I beseech you, belongs to the preceding
admonition, adding to it the force of a painfully
agitated, affectionate, and loving heart. — **You did
me no injury.**   I have no personal ground of
complaint.   This explanation agrees best with
what follows.   Paul reminds the readers of the
happy relation which existed between them at
his first visit, where they showed him the most
tender affection and were ready for any sacrifice.
— Other explanations : (1.) My severe language
(ver. 11) proceeds from no provocation of yours.
(2.) You have not offended *me* by your apostasy,
but God and Christ.   (3.) You have not injured
me, but yourselves.   (4.) I will forgive and forget all the past injury, if you now return.   (5.)
You never disobeyed me before, do not disobey
me now.

Ver. 13. **But ye know that on account of an
infirmity of the flesh I preached the gospel unto
you the former time.**   'On account of' or 'because of' is the only correct translation of the
Greek text,[1] not 'through' (as in the E. V.), nor
'in,' nor 'amid.'   The infirmity, whatever it was,
is here represented as the occasion of Paul's
preaching (not as the condition during his preaching).   It seems that he intended first merely to
pass through Galatia, on his second large missionary tour, but was detained there by some undefined bodily infirmity or sickness, and thus induced to preach the gospel.   This would place the
love of the Galatians to him in a still stronger
light, since he had no claim upon it, and became
their benefactor, so to speak, only by accident.
Conybeare well expresses the sense by translating,
somewhat too freely : 'On the contrary, although
it was sickness (as you know) which caused me
to preach the glad-tidings to you at my first visit,
yet you neither scorned nor loathed the bodily
infirmity which was my [your] trial.'   In the absence of further information, the exact character
of this infirmity of the flesh cannot be determined,
except that it was a painful, recurrent, and repulsive physical malady, no doubt the same which he
calls a 'thorn in the flesh,' 2 Cor. xii. 7   This infirmity was a check upon spiritual pride and kept

[1] Διά with the accusative, not with the genitive. Sometimes the preposition with the accusative has the temporal
sense ('during a period of sickness'), but only in poetry and
rarely.

Paul near the cross. God overruled the obstacle for the furtherance of the gospel (as He did afterwards his bonds, Phil. i. 12), and manifested the strength of His supernatural grace in and through the weakness of nature, comp. 2 Cor. xii. 9: (My) strength is made perfect in weakness. See *Excursus* below. — 'The former time,' on the first of my two visits. Paul had been twice in Galatia before writing this Epistle, comp. Acts xvi. 6; xviii. 23. At his second visit (Acts xviii. 23) the pleasant relation was already disturbed by the intermeddling of the Judaizing teachers, as intimated in ver. 16.

Ver. 14. **And your trial in my flesh ye did not scorn, nor loathe** (lit. 'spit out,' comp. Rev. iii. 16). '*Your* trial' is better supported than '*my* trial.' The infirmity of Paul tried the patience and love of the Galatians and tempted them to scorn and reject both him and the gospel which he preached. For the natural man is always disposed to judge from outward appearance. — **But ye received me as an angel of God, (even) as Christ Jesus,** who is much superior to any angel. The Galatians acted according to Matt. x. 40: 'He that receiveth you, receiveth Me, and he that receiveth Me, receiveth Him that sent Me.'

Ver. 15. **Where**[1] **is now your self-congratulation (or, your felicitation of yourselves)?** What has become of the boasting of your blessedness, of your rejoicing in my teaching, since you turned away from the freedom of the gospel to the slavery of the law? Have you the same reason now to congratulate yourselves and enjoy that beatitude, which you felt at the time of your first love, when you were ready to make the greatest sacrifices for me in return for the benefit of the gospel? The Apostle asks this question with painful affection to make the readers feel ashamed. Other explanations: (1.) **What**[2] **then [was] your self-congratulation!** *i. e.,* How hollow and unmeaning was your boast of happiness in view of your speedy apostasy! (2.) **Why, then, did you think yourselves so happy?** Answer: On account of the free grace of the gospel. (3.) **How great was your happiness!** (Ungrammatical on account of the particle and the meaning of the noun.) — **You would have plucked out your eyes and given (them) to me.** (Literally, without the ἄν, **Having plucked out your eyes you gave (them) to me.** The Greek more vividly indicates the *certainty* of the deed if it had been possible and profitable to Paul.) You were ready to make the greatest sacrifice to relieve my sufferings. The eyes are universally regarded as the most precious member of the body. Comp. Ps. xvii. 8: 'Keep me as the apple of the eye;' Deut. xxxii. 10; Prov. vii. 2. Hence the expression, 'dear as the apple of the eye.' The emphasis lies on 'eyes,' not on 'your' ('your *own*' is an interpolation of the E. V.). No inference can be drawn from this passage that Paul's infirmity consisted in disease of the eyes (acute ophthalmia), as if to say: 'Ye would have replaced my diseased eyes with your healthy eyes, if it had been possible.' Such a sacrifice would have been morally impossible, because barbarous, absurd, and useless, and not permissible by Paul.

Ver. 16. **So then have I become your enemy by telling you the truth?** He puts the conclusion politely and delicately in the form of a question instead of direct assertion. Others translate: 'Therefore (because ye loved me so much) I have become (in the opinion of the Judaizing teachers) your enemy — by telling you the truth.' In the Judaizing pseudo - Clementine writings Paul is called an 'enemy,' and 'lawless' or 'antinomian.' Some substitute 'hateful to you' for 'your enemy' (taking the Greek word in the passive sense, as Rom. v. 10; xi. 18). 'By telling you the truth,' refers to the second visit of Paul (Acts xviii. 23), when the Judaizers had probably already done much mischief.

Ver. 17. Warning against the errorists on account of their selfish exclusiveness and party spirit. **They court you,** the Judaizers (i. 7; v. 10) pay you every attention and are very busy to win you over to their party and their creed, but **not well,** in no good, honest way, not from unselfish love to you; **nay, they desire to exclude you,** or to shut you out from me and virtually from Christ Himself, by insisting on ceremonial observances as necessary to salvation; **that ye may court them,** they wish selfishly to monopolize your esteem and affection. Zeal is no test of sound doctrine, but sound doctrine must prove the zeal. Zeal without knowledge is like a sword in the hands of a madman.

Ver. 18. **It is good to be zealously courted in a good cause at all times, and not only when I am present with you.** I do not object to kind attentions and zealous devotion, provided it be from pure motives and in an honorable cause; I myself received your warmest affection during my personal presence; I only wish you would not grow cold and indifferent during my absence. This interpretation suits the tender appeal which follows.

Vers. 19 and 20. Affectionate appeal to the feelings of the Galatians. Ver. 19 may be connected with ver. 18, and a comma put after 'you,' or with ver. 20 (in which case it is difficult to explain the particle δέ in ver. 20), or may be taken as an independent sentence, an exclamation. The sense is the same. — **My little children, of whom I am again in travail,** as a mother in child-birth. The diminutive 'little' (frequently used by John, but only here by Paul) expresses more forcibly the tenderness of Paul and the feebleness of the Galatians. Usually he represents his relation to his converts as that of a spiritual *father*, 1 Cor. iv. 15; 1 Thess. ii. 11; Phil. ii. 22; Philem. ver. 10. 'Again' is used with reference to the apostasy of the Galatians so that they need a second regeneration, or conversion rather from the Judaizing pseudo-gospel to the genuine Pauline gospel, as distinct from their first conversion from heathenism to Christianity. The language is figurative and must not be pressed for dogmatic purposes. Strictly speaking, there can be but one regeneration or spiritual birth, which is the act of God, as there can be but one natural birth. But conversion, which is the act of man in turning from sin to God, may be repeated; hence the frequent exhortations in the Bible. — **Until Christ be formed in you,** as the embryo is developed into the full-grown child. We expect for 'Christ,' the 'new man;' but Christ in us is the new man, who lives and moves in us as an indwelling and all-controlling power and principle; comp. ii. 20 (and note there); Eph. iii. 17; iv. 13. Regeneration is a transplanting of Christ's life in us, a repetition, as it were, of the incarnation.

---

[1] Πού, according to the reading of the oldest and best MSS.

[2] According to the received text which reads τίς for πού, and inserts ἦν after οὖν.

Ver. 20. **But (or, yea) I could wish to be present with you now, and to change my voice,** to adapt my speech more fully to your present condition and wants, to use severity or gentle persuasion as may be best (comp. 1 Cor. iv. 21). Others: to change my present tone from severity to gentleness, to mitigate the effect of my written rebuke (comp. 2 Cor. ii. 5 ff.). But the former interpretation better suits the following clause. His wish to visit the Galatians again, was never gratified as far as we know. — **For I am perplexed about you.** I am at a loss how to address you, I know not what to think of you, I cannot understand your conduct. He fears the worst, yet hopes for the best.

PAUL'S THORN IN THE FLESH.

Excursus on Chap. IV. 13–15.   Comp. 2 Cor. xii. 7–9.[1]

Paul did his great work in constant struggle against trials and difficulties from without and from within. His life was a continuous battle with Jews, Gentiles, and false brethren. He stood almost alone, one against a world in arms. Not even a wife, or a son, or a daughter cheered him on his way, or shared with him his troubles and cares. But he had Christ on his side, who is mightier than the host of hell. This warlike aspect gives to his work the character of a heroic poem.

Among the difficulties which Paul had to contend with was that mysterious 'infirmity of the flesh,' to which he alludes in the fourth chapter of the Galatians, and the 'thorn in the flesh,' of which he speaks in the twelfth chapter of the Second Corinthians. These Epistles were written in the same period of his life (A. D. 54 to 57), and the passages refer no doubt to the same trouble. We will place them beside each other.

GAL. iv. 13–15.	2 COR. xii. 7–9.
'Ye know that on account of an infirmity of the flesh I preached unto you the former time [on the first of my two visits among you] ; and your trial in my flesh [that which was a trial to you in my flesh] ye did not scorn, nor loathe [*lit.* spit out], but as an angel of God did ye receive me, [even] as Jesus Christ. Where is then your self-congratulation ? for I bear you witness that you would have plucked out your eyes, if possible, and given them to me.'	'And that I might not be exalted too much by this superabundance of revelations, there was given to me a thorn in the flesh, an angel of Satan to buffet me, that I should not be exalted too much. For this thrice did I entreat the Lord that it might depart from me. But he hath said unto me: "My grace is sufficient for thee ; for my strength is being perfected in weakness." Most gladly then will I rather glory in my weaknesses, that the strength of Christ may rest upon me.'

The first attack of which we are informed took place fourteen years before the composition of the Second Corinthians (57), that is, A. D. 43 or 44, probably after that trance in the Temple of Jerusalem which determined his career as the Apostle of the Gentiles, 2 Cor. xii. 2 ; comp. Acts xxii. 17. Then again he was seized by a prolonged attack in 51 or 52, during his first visit to Galatia, Gal. iv. 13. He seems to refer to a similar attack, when in 52 or 53 he wrote to the Thessalonians (1 Thess. ii. 18) that 'Satan had hindered him' from visiting them, and when a few years afterwards (57) he reminded the Corinthians that he was with them 'in weakness and in fear, and in much trembling' (1 Cor. ii. 3). In the second Epistle he informs them of an affliction which befell him in Asia and which was so severe that he 'despaired even of life' (2 Cor. i. 8, 9). If we press the words 'thrice I prayed the Lord,' we may infer that down to the year 57 he had at least three severe attacks of this peculiar infirmity, and that it was after the third that the Lord pointed out to him the practical design of the trial and assured him of grace sufficient to bear it.

Allusions to the same trouble, but less certain, have been found in other passages where Paul speaks more generally of his sufferings in the cause of Christ, and more particularly his persecutions, namely, Gal. vi. 17 (the sacred stigmata or marks of Jesus branded on his body) ; 2 Cor. iv. 10 ('always bearing about in the body the dying of Jesus, that the life also of Jesus may be manifested in our body') ; Col. i. 24 ('I rejoice in my sufferings for your sake, and fill up on my part the deficiencies of the afflictions of Christ in my flesh for His body, which is the church').

The contemporaries of St. Paul who were personally acquainted with him knew at once what he meant by his 'infirmity' and by his 'thorn in the flesh ;' but we who live at such a distance are largely left to conjecture as to its precise nature. The apocryphal literature is silent on this point. The 'Acts of Thecla' give us a description of the personal appearance of Paul, but no account of his special infirmity. The magnifying glass of the legend enhances only the virtues of its heroes, while the defects disappear or are remembered only indistinctly. There is, however, a vague tradition, first briefly mentioned by Tertullian, that Paul suffered from severe headache.

What we can gather with some degree of certainty from his Epistles are the following particulars : —

1. The infirmity of Paul was a *bodily* ailment or *physical* malady. It was an 'infirmity *of the flesh*,'

---

[1] Comp. Dean Stanley, *Com. on Corinth.* (2 Cor. xii.), pp. 547–552 (4th ed. 1876). Bp. Lightfoot, *Com. on Gal.*, Excursus, pp. 183–188. Thomas Lewin, *Life and Epistles of St. Paul*, (1875) i. 186–189. Canon Farrar, *Life and Work of St. Paul*, i. 652–661. J. J. Lias, *Com. on Second Corinth.*, xii. 7. ('Cambridge Bible,' 1879). Dr. Plumptre, *Com. on Second Corinth.*, xii. 7 (in Ellicott's *N. T. Com.*).
Among older commentators, Poole, Calov, and Wolf have collected the various interpretations. Meyer gives only a brief summary on 2 Cor. xii., pp. 337, 338 (fifth Germ. ed., 1870).

Gal. iv. 13, or 'in his (my) flesh,' ver. 14, 'a thorn in the flesh,' 2 Cor. xii. 7, that is, not a literal thorn, but a physical pain, as sharp as that caused by a thorn or pin thrust in the flesh.[1] It is true, 'flesh' often means, in Paul's vocabulary, the corrupt carnal nature of man, but in these passages it must refer to the body; for a check on the sinful nature would be a spiritual blessing rather than a hindrance to get rid of.

2. It must have been very *painful*. This is implied in the Greek word σκόλοψ, which only occurs once in the New Testament, but frequently elsewhere, and means either a wooden 'stake,' or a sharp 'thorn,' a splinter; the latter meaning prevails in Hellenistic Greek (LXX. Hos. ii. 6; Ezek. xxviii. 24; Num. xxxiii. 55; Sir. xliii. 19), and is decidedly preferable here, for the idea of a stake driven through the flesh is exaggerated and coarse.[2] The Apostle moreover prayed again and again to be delivered from this pain. A man of his energy and zeal would not have minded or mentioned an ordinary ailment.

3. It was of a repulsive and even *loathsome* character, and offered a strong temptation to the Galatians to 'despise' and 'spit out' the Apostle. But it created also pity and compassion on the sufferer.

4. It was not a continuous, but an *intermittent* trouble. It seized him while passing through Galatia and *detained* him there, so that he involuntarily became the evangelist and spiritual father of the Galatians, Gal. iv. 13 (according to the correct rendering of δι' ἀσθένειαν τῆς σαρκός, 'on account of an infirmity of the flesh'). The intermittent character is also implied in the word 'buffet.'

5. It was not hereditary, but dated, it would seem, from the time of his conversion or afterwards; as Jacob's lameness came from his wrestling with Jehovah. He says : ' There was *given* to me (ἐδόθη) a thorn in the flesh.' And it was given to him by God through Satan for his humiliation. It is possible, however, that the disease dated from the earlier life of Paul, and was aggravated and also graciously overruled after his conversion.

6. It had a mysterious background, and was connected with *demoniac* influences ; for he describes the trouble as an 'angel of Satan,'[3] who did 'buffet' him or strike him with the fist. But Satan was here, as in the case of Job, only an instrument in the hands of the permissive and overruling providence of God, and had to serve against his will the moral end of guarding the Apostle against spiritual pride.

7. It was apt to break out after some special *revelation* or exaltation with which Paul was favored from time to time. For he mentions it after the account of his rapture into the third heaven where he heard 'unspeakable words which it is not lawful for a man to utter,' and he represents the thorn in the flesh as a counter-action to the inflation and boastfulness which such exceptional insight into the mysteries of divine truth might otherwise have produced. Sudden transitions from a taste of heavenly glory to earthly misery are not infrequent in the lives of saints. The disciples had to come down from the Mount of Transfiguration to be confronted with hideous maladies, — a contrast so admirably reproduced by Raphael in his last and greatest picture. Peter after he had, by revelation, confessed Christ as the Son of God, and earned the name of ' Rock,' was rebuked and called ' Satan,' because, under the influence of his flesh and blood, if not of Satan himself, he had, presumed to warn his Lord and Master against the path of suffering which alone could lead to the redemption of the world.

So far exegesis may go with the data before us. Some of the ablest commentators stop here, and say that Paul's infirmity was a painful physical malady which he derived from Satan, but which cannot now be definitely determined.[4]

But it is very interesting to examine the various theories and conjectures. Some are fanciful, some probable, none certain. They reflect the various personal experiences and trials of Christian men. We may classify them under three heads: physical evils ; external calamities ; spiritual trials.

I. PHYSICAL MALADIES.

Almost every ailment or disorder to which human flesh is subject has been named by commentators as the thorn in the flesh, such as headache, earache, blindness, or sore eyes, dyspepsia, gravel, epilepsy, hypochondria, impediment of speech, diminutive figure, nervous prostration, a general sickly condition (rather than a particular disease), but those only deserve special consideration which combine more or less the characteristic features which are required by the text. These are ophthalmia, epilepsy, and sick headache.

1. *Inflammation of the eyes*, or *acute ophthalmia*.[5] This disease is still very prevalent in the Orient, especially in Egypt, among children and adults, and often presents an aspect almost as distressing as leprosy and epilepsy. In every street of Alexandria and Cairo, you may see children suffering with eyes inflamed and besieged by flies, on the arms or shoulders of the mother, who from superstitious fear of evil spirits makes no attempt to drive the flies away. The Egyptian ophthalmia, so called, is contagious and accompanied by severe burning pain, headache, and prostration. ' When the disease is unchecked, it is liable to produce ulceration or sloughing of the cornea, with the escape of the aqueous humor and protrusion of the iris ; and even when these results do not follow, vision is often destroyed by permanent opacity of the cornea.'

---

[1] The dative τῇ σαρκί, 2 Cor. xii. 7, is the dative of appropriation, 'a thorn for the flesh.' So Meyer *in loc.*, but he misunderstands σάρξ of that part of the spiritual man which is most inclined to sin. This is inconsistent with the 'infirmity *of* the flesh' in Gal., and Paul would not have prayed for a removal of a check on his sinful inclination.

[2] Against Lightfoot, Plumptre, and Farrar, who all prefer the meaning ' stake,' misled by the prevailing classical usage The Vulgate translates σκόλοψ by *stimulus*.

[3] Ἄγγελος Σατανᾶ is in apposition to σκόλοψ. Satan has under him a host of fallen angels, Matt. xxv. 41, and uses them as agents for all sorts of evil and mischief of which he is the prime author, comp. 1 Cor. ii. 12; 2 Cor. iv. 4; xi. 14; 1 Thess. ii. 18, etc., and also Job ii. 3 ff.

[4] So Olshausen, De Wette, Meyer, Neander, Stanley, and others.

[5] So very positively Lewin, Plumptre, Farrar, and other English and American writers. It is strange that Meyer in his summary of views does not even mention the theory of ophthalmia.

In favor of this theory the following arguments have been urged, none of which, however, is conclusive : —

(*a*.) Paul was struck with blindness by the dazzling light of glory which appeared to him at his conversion. But this blindness lasted only three days, and was — as it would seem, permanently — cured by Ananias, Acts ix. 8, 9, 17, 18.

(*b*.) The Galatians in the first flush of their gratitude for Paul, who, notwithstanding his severe affliction, preached to them the good tidings of salvation, were willing, if possible, to *pluck out* even their *eyes* [1] and to give them to the suffering messenger of God, Gal. iv. 15. But the eyes, the most precious members of the body, represent here figuratively the greatest sacrifice.

(*c*.) Paul did not recognize the high-priest, when he called him a 'whited wall,' Acts xxiii. 3-5. But this may have been owing to nearsightedness, rather than to diseased vision.

(*d*.) His handwriting was awkward, Gal. vi. 11 ('See what large letters, or characters, I write with mine own hand '), and he usually employed an amanuensis, Rom. xvi. 22. But the former passage refers only to the large *size* of the letters, which is often characteristic of boldness ; and even bad and illegible handwriting is not infrequent among men of genius with sound eyes.

(*e*.) The term 'thorn in the flesh ' naturally suggests the image of a sharp splinter run into the eye, and an ocular deformity caused thereby, which might well be compared to the brand fixed on a slave, Gal. vi. 17. But this passage refers to permanent marks of persecution from without rather than an inherent trouble.

If Paul suffered from blindness, or blurred vision, he would involuntarily remind us of the two greatest epic poets, — Homer and Milton, — of the eminent divine Dionysius of Alexandria, and of the historian Prescott. His vision of the outward world was dimmed that he might see the mysteries of the spiritual and eternal world. Milton wrote his ' Paradise Lost ' and 'Paradise Regained ' in midnight darkness, yet full of faith and hope : —

> 'These eyes,
> Bereft of light, their seeing have forgot ;
> Nor to their idle orbs doth sight appear
> Of sun, or moon, or star, throughout the year,
> Or man, or woman. Yet I argue not
> Against Heaven's hand and will, nor bate a jot
> Of heart or hope, but still bear up, and steer
> Right onward.' [2]

2. *Epilepsy*, or *the falling sickness*.[3] This answers nearly every condition of the text. It is painful ; it is recurrent ; it suspends all voluntary action ; it is exceedingly humiliating, distressing, and repulsive, and makes the sufferer an object of loathing to others. It is often connected with delicate sensibility, nervous excitement, visions, and trances. It is characterized by sudden insensibility, spasmodic movements of the muscles, violent distortions of the face, protrusion of the tongue, foaming at the mouth, and ghastly expression of countenance. The fits last usually from five to twenty minutes and are followed by a state of stupor. Epilepsy was considered by the ancients as a supernatural and 'sacred disease,' and derived from the influence of the gods or evil spirits ; the Jews traced it to demoniacal possession ; the Welsh call it ' the rod of Christ.' Mohammed often had trances and epileptic fits, during which he foamed at the mouth, and uttered guttural sounds like a camel ; at first he and his followers derived them from evil spirits, but afterwards from the angel Gabriel who inspired his messages. The faintings and ecstasies of St. Bernard, St. Francis of Assisi, St. Catherine of Siena, St. Teresa of Spain, George Fox, and Emanuel Swedenborg may also be mentioned as illustrations or analogies. Recent English commentators have called attention to the case of King Alfred, the greatest and best of English kings. It is said that God sent him in his youth a malady which had all the symptoms of epilepsy, in answer to the prayer for some corporal suffering or other protection against the temptations of the flesh. For many years it caused him terrible tortures and led him to despair of his life, but then it left him, in answer to his fervent prayers for deliverance, until it suddenly reappeared in the midst of his marriage festival, to the dismay of the guests, and rudely silenced their loud joy. To a good old age he was never sure against its recurrence, and it was under the load of this bodily infirmity that he discharged, most energetically and faithfully, the duties of a sovereign in a most trying time.[4] I knew an eminent and celebrated Christian scholar of high moral and religious character, who in his younger years was subject to this terrible disease ; but his friends concealed it.

The only serious objection to this theory is the repulsive character of epilepsy. But Paul himself describes his infirmity as loathsome. It is also urged that he must have had a powerful constitution to make so many journeys by land and by sea, to preach in the day and to work at his trade in the night, and to endure all sorts of hardship and persecution. But physical infirmity is sometimes combined with great nervous vitality and tenacity.

3. *Sick headache.* This has in its favor the oldest tradition. It is first mentioned by Tertullian, who adds to it earache,[5] and is confirmed by Jerome, who mentions the traditional report that Paul often suffered the most severe headache.[6] I would unhesitatingly adopt this view if it were not for the objection that headache, even in its severest form, does not present the feature of such repulsiveness as to make the sufferer an object of contempt. As the argument now stands, the second theory has, exegetically, the advantage above all others.

---

[1] Not ' your *own* eyes,' as King James' version has it. The Greek ὑμῶν is not emphatic, and the stress lays on eyes,' not on 'your.'

[2] I may mention, as instances, Napoleon, Neander, Dean Stleany.

[3] Ziegler, Ewald ('*fallende Sucht oder so was ähnliches*'), Hausrath, Holsten, and especially Lightfoot.

[4] Pauli's *Life of Alfred*, Engl. transl., pp. 122-125, quoted by Jowett and Lightfoot.

[5] *De Pudic.*, c. 13 : '*per dolorem, ut aiunt, auriculæ vel capitis.*'

[6] *Com. in Gal.* iv. 14 : '*Tradunt eum gravissimum capitis dolorem sæpe perpessum.*' Chrysostom, Theophylact, Pelagius, and Œcumenius likewise mention this opinion as held by some (τινές).

4

II.   EXTERNAL TROUBLES.

These are ruled out by the text which points to an *inherent* difficulty inseparable from his *person*, although it was not always felt with the same force.

1. *Persecutions.*[1] Chrysostom argues, quite inconclusively: ' It cannot have been a headache as some suppose ; it cannot have been any physical malady. God would not have delivered over the body of His chosen servant to the power of the devil to be tortured in this way. The Apostle is surely speaking of opposition encountered, of suffering endured from enemies.' Paul speaks of his persecutions differently and very plainly in other passages, 2 Cor. iv. 7 ff. ; xi. 25 ff. Moreover persecution *followed* the preaching of the gospel, while the infirmity spoken of in the Galatians *preceded* the preaching.

2. *Opposition* of the *Judaizing* opponents who embittered his life and were the servants of Satan (2 Cor. xi. 13, 15), together with the cares and anxieties of his office generally.[2] A modification of the former view. No doubt the intrigues of the Judaizers and other mean people tried the Apostle very sorely, and sometimes provoked him to the use of sarcastic language, but they were necessary conditions of the development of Christian truth and of his own system of doctrine.

3. *A bad wife* (like Job's). But Paul was probably never married (1 Cor. vii. 7-9) ; and if he had been, he would certainly not have prayed for the removal of his wife. This and similar fancies are only worth mentioning as curiosities of exegesis.

III.   MORAL AND SPIRITUAL TRIALS.

1. *Carnal temptations.* Paul had to contend with a rebellious sensuality, without, however, being overcome by it. This is the ascetic explanation, vaguely suggested by Jerome, favored by the ambiguous Latin rendering of the 'thorn in the flesh ' (*stimulus carnis*), and adopted by most of the mediæval and Roman Catholic commentators. Cornelius a Lapide calls it the common interpretation of the Catholics. Cardinal Hugo fancied that the passion was stimulated by the beautiful St. Thecla, one of Paul's converts and companions (according to apocryphal accounts). Many an ascetic saint, beset by the devil in this way, derived comfort from the belief that Paul was tempted in the same way. Passages like 1 Cor. ix. 27 : ' I buffet my body, and bring it into bondage ; ' Rom. vii. 23 : ' the law of sin in my members ;' Eph. vi. 16 (the 'firetipt darts of the wicked one '), are quoted in support. But the word 'thorn' was never used of the sting of sensuous impulse. What is more conclusive, Paul says expressly with reference to marriage and carnal temptations that he wished all men were as free as he, 1 Cor. vii. 7-9. We look in vain for stronger condemnation of all impurity than in his Epistles. It is preposterous to suppose that he who was all-absorbed in the service of Christ should have been pursued by a sinful passion to such an extent as to be hindered in his ministry and to become an object of contempt and loathing to his converts. And how in the world could he glory in shameful lusts ? And how could concupiscence be a check and counter-poise to spiritual pride ?[3]

2. *Violent temper.* This does not answer the description at all. No doubt Paul, like most great men, had fiery passions, but under the control of reason, and made subservient to his work. He handled good old Peter rather severely at Antioch ; he separated even from his friend Barnabas for a while on account of Mark ; he nearly lost his temper when he reviled the high priest ; and his Epistles generally are full of sacred fire. Nothing great can be done without enthusiasm, guided by reason. Strong temper is as useful as a strong physical constitution when employed in a good cause. Abuse of temper is always humiliating and a sign of weakness. But some people have no temper to control, and hence deserve no credit for moderation.

3. *Spiritual temptations,* such as doubt, despondency, faint-heartedness in his calling, torments of conscience on account of his former life, disappointed ambition, blasphemous suggestions of the devil.[4] Paul no doubt had constant conflicts with the powers of darkness, and often felt weary of the strife, and home-sick after heaven (comp. 2 Cor. v. 1-5; Phil. i. 23 ; 2 Tim. iv. 6), but he never shows the least misgiving as to his faith and his ministry. Having seen the Lord personally, and having been favored repeatedly with special revelations, he would rather have doubted his own existence than the truth of the gospel or his duty as an Apostle.

PRACTICAL LESSONS.

1. Paul's 'thorn in the flesh,' no matter what it was, heightens our conception of his heroism and all-absorbing devotion to Christ, for whom he was ready to suffer all things and to sacrifice life itself.

2. The diversity of interpretations arises from the want of definite information and reflects the personal experiences and trials of the commentators. The impossibility of attaining at a certain result facilitates the applicability and practical usefulness of that undefined 'infirmity.'

[1] Chrysostom and other Greek commentators. Augustin is also quoted in favor of this view, but he suggested different conjectures and had no fixed opinion on this subject.

[2] Theodoret, Erasmus, Calvin, Beza, Schrader, Reiche, etc.

[3] Meyer calls this Roman interpretation ' a crime against the great Apostle.' But it is psychologically interesting, as showing that excruciating carnal temptations may enter into the experience of earnest monks, priests, and holy men. St. Jerome speaks of them rather indelicately in letters to female friends, whom he exhorts to keep the vow of chastity. St. Augustin bewails the recurrence in dreams of the old sensuous pictures after his conversion.

[4] So Gerson, Luther, Calov, Mosheim, and others. Luther often had Satanic suggestions, and traced the gravel, which troubled him very much, to the devil. In his earlier commentary on Gal. (1519), he explained Paul's infirmity with Chrysostom of persecutions; in his fuller commentary (1535), he added high spiritual temptations; and lastly in his *Table-Talk*, he mentions the latter only.

3. Every Christian has a 'thorn in his flesh,' either physical, or spiritual, or external. Some have more than one. It may be sickness, or poverty, or misfortune, or persecution, or doubt, or despondency, or unruly temper, or a bad husband, a bad wife, bad children, or any other kind of trouble.

4. The object and use of a thorn in the flesh is to keep us humble and near the cross. It is a check to pride, vanity, sensuality, and other sins. Human nature is too weak to stand uninterrupted prosperity without injury.

5. The thorn in the flesh aids us in developing the passive virtues, meekness, gentleness, patience, resignation. We are often laid on the back that we may learn to look up to heaven. When Paul was weakest in the flesh, he was strongest in spirit. 'And what his trial was to him and to the world on a large scale, that the trial of each individual Christian may have been ever since, the means, in ways inconceivable to him now, of making himself and others strong in the service of God and man.'[1]

6. The comfort in answer to our prayers for deliverance from our thorn in the flesh is that which was given to Paul : 'My grace is sufficient for thee ; for (My) strength is made perfect in weakness.' The same answer, though we hear it not, is returned to us in similar trials. Prayer is often refused in one form, but answered in a far better form than we can conceive. The cross of Christ is the strength of Christianity.[2]

Continuation of the Argument by a Biblical Allegory.

CHAPTER IV. 21-31.

The Apostle resumes his argument for the superiority of the gospel over the law, and illustrates the difference of the two by an allegorical interpretation of the history of Sarah and Hagar, and their sons.

21 TELL me, ye that desire to be under the law,[1] do ye not
22 hear the law ?[2] For it is written that Abraham had two *a* Gen. xvi. 15.
23 sons, *a* the one by a[3] bondmaid, *b* the other by a free woman.[4] *b* Gen. xxi. 2, *c* Rom. ix. 7, 8.
But he *who was* of the bondwoman[5] *c* was born after the flesh ; *d* Gen. xviii.
24 *d* but he of the free woman[6] *was* by promise.[7] Which things 10, 14; xxi. 1, 2; Heb. xi. 11.
are an allegory :[8] for these[9] are the[10] two covenants ; the one
from the[11] mount *e* Sinai, which gendereth to bondage,[12] which *e* Deut. xxxiii. 2.
25 is Agar.[13] For this Agar is mount Sinai in Arabia,[14] and an-
swereth to Jerusalem[15] which now is, and is[16] in bondage with
26 her children. But[17] *f* Jerusalem which is above is free, which is *f* Is. ii. 2; Heb. xii. 22; Rev. iii. 12; xxi. 2, 10.
27 the mother of us all.[18] For it is written, *g* Isa. liv. 1.

  g 'Rejoice, thou barren that bearest not ;

  'Break forth and cry, thou that travailest not :

[1] or, under law   [2] Law   [3] the
[4] the freewoman   [5] the *son* from the bondmaid
[6] the *son* from the free woman   [7] *is* through the promise
[8] are allegorized   [9] these *women*   [10] *omit* the
[11] *omit* the   [12] bringing forth unto bondage   [13] and this is Hagar
[14] *Some of the best authorities omit* Hagar, *and read*, For Sinai is a mountain in Arabia. *The clause should be enclosed in parentheses.*
[15] correspondeth to the Jerusalem   [16] for she is   [17] the
[18] and she is our mother

[1] Stanley.
[2] Compare the couplet of Schiller (his best):—

        'Religion des Kreuzes nur du verknüpfest in Einem Kranze
        Der Demuth und Kraft doppelte Palme zugleich.'

' For the desolate hath many more children
' Than she which hath a husband.' [19]

28 Now we,[20] brethren, as Isaac was, are [h] the [21] children of prom-   [h] Acts iii. 25; Rom. ix. 8;

29 ise. But as then [i] he that was born after the flesh persecuted   [i] chap. iii. 29. Gen. xxi. 9.

30 him *that was born* after the Spirit, [k] even so *it is* [22] now. Never-   [k] Chap. v. 11; vi. 12.

theless what saith [l] the Scripture?   [l] Chap. iii. 8, 22.

[m] ' Cast out the bondwoman [23] and her son : for [n] the son of   [m] GEN. xxi. 10, 12.

the bondwoman shall not be heir [24] with the son of the free   [n] John viii. 35.

31 woman.' [25] So then, [26] brethren, we are not children of the [27]   [o] John viii. 36; chap. v. 1, 13.

bondwoman, [o] but of the free.[28]

[19] Many *are* the children of the desolate,
More than of her who hath the husband

[20] But ye   [21] *omit* the   [22] omit *it is*

[23] bondmaid (*as in vers.* 21 *and* 22)   [24] shall in no wise inherit

[25] freewoman   [26] Wherefore (*according to the most approved reading,* διό)

[27] a   [28] the freewoman

Ver. 21. **Tell me.** This makes the question more urgent and compels the Judaizing Galatians to an evangelical answer. — **Ye that desire to be under law, do ye not hear the Law?** Ye who are so anxious to live under the power and authority of the legal dispensation, will ye not listen to the lesson of the book of the Law? Comp. Matt. xiii. 13; xxiv. 15; Luke xvi. 29. Others take it as a question of astonishment! Is not the Law (which ought to convince you of your error) constantly read in your synagogues? Comp. Luke iv. 16; John xii. 32; Acts xv. 21; 2 Cor. iii. 14. The law in the first clause means the legal institute and authority; the Law in the second clause designates, as often, the Pentateuch (the *Thora*), as distinct from the Prophets (*Nebiim*), and the remaining sacred writings (*Chetubim* or *Hagiographa*).

Ver. 22. **Abraham had two sons, one by the bondmaid, the other by the freewoman.** See Gen. xvi. 1 ff.; xxi. 1 ff. The 'bondmaid' is Hagar, the 'freewoman' is Sarah. In the national legends of the Mohammedan Arabs who derive their descent from Ishmael, Hagar is represented as the lawful wife, and Ishmael as the legitimate son of Abraham; they settled in Mecca and were refreshed from the well in the holy Kaaba, which was from time immemorial and is to this day a sanctuary and resort of pilgrimage. The Mohammedans pray five times a day with their face turned to Mecca. It is remarkable how the relation of Ishmael to Abraham has been perpetuated in history. The Mohammedans are in their religion genuine Ishmaelites, bastard Jews, and wild sons of the desert, whose hands are against every man. (Gen. xvi. 12.)

Ver. 23. **But the son from the bondmaid was born after the flesh,** in the regular course of nature. (Used somewhat differently in Rom. i. 3 and ix. 5.) **But the son of the freewoman is through the promise,** by virtue of supernatural influence, by the Spirit of God working through the word of promise (as in the conception of our Lord). Gen. xvii. 16, 19; xviii. 10, 11; comp. Rom. iv. 19.

Ver. 24. **Which things are allegorized,** allegor-ically expounded, have an allegorical signification. The story of Hagar and Sarah has another (namely, a figurative, typical) meaning, besides (not, instead of) the literal or historical. Paul does not deny the fact, but makes it the bearer of a general idea, which was more fully expressed in two covenants. He uses allegorical here in a sense similar to the word 'typical' in 1 Cor. x. 11 (Greek). See the *Excursus.* 'Allegory' means a description of one thing under the figure of another, so that the *real* or intended meaning differs from the *obvious* sense of the words; the verb 'to allegorize' (only used here in the New Testament) means, (1) to speak in an allegory or figuratively, that is so as to intend another sense than the words express; (2) to interpret as an allegory, and in the passive mood: to have an allegorical meaning. So here. — **For these** (two women, Hagar and Sarah) **are two covenants.** They 'are' allegorically, that is, they represent or signify, two covenants. Comp. Matt. xiii. 39; xxvi. 26-28; 1 Cor. x. 4. — **One** (of them) **from Mount Sinai, bringing forth** (or bearing children) **unto bondage; and this is Hagar.** The regular antithesis would be : 'the other from Mount Sion (which corresponds to the upper Jerusalem), bearing children unto freedom; and this is Sarah.' This is substantially expressed in ver. 26, but owing to the intervening explanatory parenthesis, ver. 25, the grammatical form melts away in the general structure. Besides the parallel is not quite complete; for Sarah was the mother not only of the true spiritual children of Abraham, but also of those carnal Jews who are no better than the children of Hagar, who strictly speaking stood outside of the Sinaitic covenant and became through her illegitimate son Ishmael the mother of a bastard Judaism (the religion of Mohammed).

Ver. 25. A difficult passage. The reading of the first clause is disputed. The longer text (which is supported by the Vatican MS. and adopted by Westcott and Hort) reads : **But** (or, **Now**) **this Hagar is Mount Sinai in Arabia.**[1] This implies

[1] A, B, D, E read τὸ τὸ δὲ Αγαρ Σινᾶ ὄρος ἐστίν ἐν τῇ Αρα-βίᾳ. K, L, P, with the majority of cursive MSS., read γάρ (*for*) instead of δέ (*but, now*).

that the name Hagar was an Arabic designation for Mount Sinai, but this cannot be satisfactorily proven (as the testimonies of Chrysostom and the Bohemian traveller Harant are isolated and unconfirmed). Hagar means 'Wanderer,' 'Fugitive,' and is connected with the Arabic 'Hegira' (the famous 'flight' of Mohammed from Mecca to Medina, whence the beginning of the Mohammedan era) ; Sinai means 'Pointed,' or (according to Fürst) 'Rocky.' There is, however, an Arabic word of similar sound, though different etymology, (' Hadschar,' or 'Hadjar,' 'Chajar'), which means a 'stone' or a 'rock,' and is to this day applied to several remarkable stones on and around Sinai, *e. g.* to the traditional rock from which Moses drew water (in the Wady Leja). At the time of Paul, who was himself in Arabia (see note on i. 17), it may have been (and in case this reading is correct, it *must* have been) a local name of one of the peaks of that group of barren rocks, or of the whole group ; as 'Selah' or 'Petra' ('Rock') was the name of the famous rock-hewn city, in the Sinaitic Peninsula, and that part of Arabia was called the 'Rocky Arabia' (*Arabia Petræa*). At present the principal peaks of Sinai are called 'Jebel Musa' (Mount of Moses, the *traditional* mount of legislation), 'Ras Sufsâfeh' (the *probable* mount of legislation, facing the vast plain Er Raha), and 'Jebel Katharina.' Calvin and others escape this difficulty by explaining : 'Hagar is *a type of* (or, *represents*) Mount Sinai in Arabia.' But against this is the Greek neuter article before Hagar ('the *thing*' or 'the *name*' Hagar ; not in the feminine, 'the *woman* Hagar'). The shorter reading (of the Sinaitic MS. and the Vulgate, adopted by Lachmann, Tischendorf, in the last edition, and Lightfoot) is : **For Sinai is a mountain in Arabia.**[1] This is quite intelligible and free from the difficulty just mentioned, though for this very reason subject to the suspicion of being a correction, if it were not for the ease with which the insertion of Hagar can be explained in the Greek. Some take the clause in either case as a parenthesis, others as a continuation of the argument. It cannot be merely a geographical notice for the Galatians ; for Sinai was well known to all who had heard of the Mosaic legislation. The stress seems to lie on 'Arabia,' known as a land of the wild descendants of Hagar. She fled with Ishmael to the Sinaitic Peninsula (Gen. xvi. 7, 14) ; several Arab tribes were named after her 'Hagarenes' or 'Hagarites' (Ps. lxxxiii. 7 ; I Chr. v. 19), and the Arabs generally were called 'sons of Hagar' (Baruch iii. 23). The law was given not on Mount Sion in the land of promise, but outside of it in Arabia, and this corresponds to Hagar who was an outsider, an Egyptian slave. The law 'came in beside' (iii. 19 ; Rom. v. 20), and had only an intermediate and transitory importance in the history of salvation. — **Correspondeth to the Jerusalem which now is.** Lit. : belongs to the same row or column, is in the same rank with. Both have the same nature, namely, both are in bondage. But what is the subject of the verb ? If the preceding clause be taken as a parenthesis, the subject is the Sinaitic covenant, ver. 24 ; but if it is not parenthetical, Hagar is the subject in the longer reading, or Mount Sinai in the shorter reading. 'The Jerusalem which

now is,' or the present, the earthly Jerusalem, which represents, as the metropolis, the whole Jewish race, the Mosaic theocracy. — **For she is in bondage with her children.** In bondage to the Mosaic law (also to Rome, although this is not meant here). The Jewish church which crucified the Lord and persecutes the Christian church, is in spiritual slavery, as Hagar was in literal slavery. We must here remember the Pauline distinction between two Israels, a spiritual Israel which embraces all believers, whether of the circumcision or of the uncircumcision, and is the true heir of promise, and the carnal Israel, which has only the circumcision of the flesh, and not of the heart, which is of the blood, but not of the faith of Abraham, and is cast out like Hagar and Ishmael. Comp. Rom. ii. 26-29 ; iv. 12 ff. ; ix. 6 ff.

Ver. 26. **But the Jerusalem which is above (or, the upper Jerusalem) is free; and she is our mother (mother of us).** The reading of the E. V. ' of us *all*' is not sufficiently supported, and arose probably at an early time from Rom. iv. 16, 'the father of us all,' or from a loose quotation of this passage by Polycarp. The other covenant, that which is represented by Sarah and her believing offspring, is the true or heavenly Jerusalem, that is not (as the rabbinical teachers imagined) an actual material city in heaven (the exact counterpart of the earthly Jerusalem), which was to be let down in the Messianic age, but a spiritual city, the Messianic theocracy, the kingdom of heaven, to which all true Christians belong, even here on earth, Phil. iii. 20. The word 'above,' therefore is not local, but ethical and spiritual ; as in the phrase, 'the kingdom of heaven,' to be born 'from above.' Comp. the 'heavenly Jerusalem,' Hebr. xii. 22 (where it is contrasted with mount Sinai, ver. 18), the 'new Jerusalem,' Rev. iii. 12 ; xxi. 2. — 'And she is our mother,' the mother of us Christians. This passage and the concluding chapters of Revelation struck the keynote to the hymn 'Mother dear, Jerusalem,' and the other New Jerusalem hymns in Latin, English, and German, which express so touchingly the Christian's longing after his eternal home in heaven.

Ver. 27. **'Rejoice, thou barren that bearest not,'** etc. An illustration of the allegory by a passage from Isa. liv. 1, which prophesies the deliverance of God's afflicted nation from the foreign bondage of the Babylonian exile, and her restoration to freedom and prosperity, so that from a mourning widow, like Sarah, she shall become a rejoicing mother of many children. The prophet himself, in a previous chapter (li. 2), refers to God's dealings with Abraham and Sarah, as a type of his dealings with their descendants. In the application, the barren who becomes fruitful, is the type of the Christian church, more especially the Gentile Christian church, as opposed to the Jewish synagogue. This application is fully justified by the Messianic character of the whole second part of Isaiah (beginning with chap. xl.).

Ver. 28. **But ye, brethren, as Isaac was (or, after the manner of Isaac), are children of promise.** Resumes the main subject ; comp. ver. 23. Christian believers are born, like Isaac, of the unfruitful Sarah, contrary to the ordinary course of nature, by the supernatural power of the divine promise, and are therefore children of the heavenly Jerusalem.

Ver. 29. **But as then he that was born after the flesh persecuted him** (*that was born*) **after the Spirit, even so now.** The history of Isaac and

Ishmael was typical also in another respect, inasmuch as it foreshadowed the hostility of the carnal, unbelieving Judaism against Christianity. 'Persecuted him.' According to the Hebrew text, Gen. xxi. 9, Ishmael was simply 'laughing' or 'mocking' at the festival in honor of the weaning of Isaac; whereupon Sarah said unto Abraham: 'Cast out this bondwoman and her son.' But the Jewish tradition expanded the word, so as to mean an assault of Ishmael upon Isaac. This insolence was repeated in the aggressions of the Arab tribes, especially the Hagarenes on the Israelites (Ps. lxxxiii. 7; 1 Chr. v. 10, 19), and on a still grander scale in the persecutions of the Mohammedans against Jews and Christians. — 'Even so (it is) now.' So now the Christian church which is born of the Spirit, is persecuted by the Jewish synagogue which is born after the flesh. And this same conduct is repeated also by the bigoted Judaizing party against the free evangelical church of the Gentiles.

Ver. 30. **Nevertheless what saith the Scripture? 'Cast out the bondmaid and her son; for the son of the bondmaid shall in no wise inherit with the son of the freewoman.'** Words of Sarah to Abraham on the occasion of the mocking of Ishmael, Gen. xxi. 10, but approved and confirmed by God, ver. 12, so that Ishmael was actually expelled from the house of Abraham. Paul quotes from the LXX., with a slight change of 'my son Isaac' into 'the son of the freewoman,' which adapts it to his argument and saves explanation. The Apostles were no slavish literalists, but used the Bible freely in the very Spirit which gave it. — 'Shall in no wise inherit.'

The double negation in Greek is emphatic: assuredly not. Judaism and Christianity, bondage and freedom, cannot exist together: the one must exclude the other.. This appears very plain to us now, but before the destruction of Jerusalem it sounded strange and incredible, at least to the Judaizers, who held on to the old traditions as long as they could. 'It is scarcely possible' (says Lightfoot) 'to estimate the strength of conviction and depth which this declaration implies. The Apostle thus confidently sounds the death-knell of Judaism at a time when one half of Christendom clung to the Mosaic law with a jealous affection little short of frenzy, and while the Judaic party seemed to be growing in influence and was strong enough, even in the Gentile churches of his own founding, to undermine his influence and endanger his life.'

Ver. 31. **Wherefore, brethren, we are not children of a (i. e. any) bondwoman, but of the free-woman.** The pith of the typological illustration, ver. 21 ff., and the final result of the whole discussion of the fourth chapter. The change of the definite and indefinite article (so often obliterated by the E. V.) is not without point. There are *many* bondwomen, false churches and sects, but only *one* freewoman, the lawful spouse of Christ, in whom all true believers are one. Some eminent commentators begin with this verse a new section, as expressing the theoretical preamble of the practical exhortation in chap. v., thus: 'Therefore, brethren, we are not children of a bondwoman (like the Jews), but of the freewoman; for (or, unto) freedom Christ hath made us free: 'stand fast, therefore,' etc. (So Meyer.)

Excursus on Allegorical and Typical Interpretation.

CHAPTER IV. 21–31.

We have here an ingenious specimen of a typical allegory. Paul represents Hagar (the slave and concubine) and Sarah (the mistress and lawful wife), with their sons, Ishmael and Isaac, as the types of two covenants, a covenant of law or bondage, and a covenant of promise or freedom. The contrast of the two mothers is reproduced in their two sons, and on a larger scale in two religions, the Jewish and the Christian. It is again repeated in the antagonism between the legalistic Jewish, and the evangelical Gentile Christianity. The points of contrast are as follows:—

HAGAR AND ISHMAEL = JUDAISM.	SARAH AND ISAAC = CHRISTIANITY.
The Old Covenant.	The New Covenant.
The Law.	The Gospel (the Promise).
Natural Birth.	Spiritual Birth.
Mount Sinai in Arabia.	(Mount Sion in the Land of Promise?)
Earthly Jerusalem.	Heavenly Jerusalem.
Bondage.	Freedom.
Persecuting.	Persecuted.
Expulsion.	Inheritance.

Paul accommodates himself here, as in two other instances (iii. 6; 1 Cor. x. 4), in some measure, but within the bounds of sobriety and legitimate application, to the prevailing rabbinical exegesis in which he was trained. He does so exceptionally and incidentally. He does not rest the truth or the argument on an allegorical interpretation, but uses it as an accessory illustration of a truth previously established by solid argument. Luther compares it to a painting which decorates a house already built.

Paul regards the patriarchal family with good reason as a miniature picture of the future history of the church, which it represented and anticipated. He does not in the least deny the historical character of Abraham, Sarah, and Hagar; but he ascribes to it, at the same time, a wider typical import, and sees in Abraham the father of the faithful, in Sarah and Hagar the mothers of two races and two covenants, in which their personal character and condition is reflected and carried out on a larger scale. This is all sound and true. The chief difficulty is in the identification of Hagar with Sinai, and this is much relieved by the shorter reading. In point of fact the law was given to the descendants of Sarah and Isaac, not to those of Hagar and Ishmael, who stood outside of the covenant. But Sarah and Isaac represented first and last the covenant of promise which overruled the interimistic covenant of law which was given in the desert borderland of the Ishmaelites, as a tutor to prepare the Israelites for the fulfilment of the promise.

Now let us compare with this Scripture passage the allegorical interpretation of the same history by the celebrated Philo of Alexandria (about A. D. 40), the master of the art of allegorizing. According to his view, Abraham represents the human soul progressing towards the knowledge of God. His first wife, Sarah, 'the princess,' represents divine wisdom. His second wife, Hagar, 'the sojourner,' the Egyptian handmaid of Sarah, means preparatory scholastic training or secular learning, which is transient and unsatisfying. His marriage with Sarah is at first premature and unfruitful; hence she directs him to cohabit with her handmaid, that is to study the lower wisdom of the schools; and the alliance proves fruitful at once. Afterwards he again unites himself to Sarah, who bears him a son with a countless offspring; thus the barren woman becomes 'most fruitful.' Moreover, Isaac likewise represents true wisdom, Ishmael sophistry, which in the end must give place to wisdom, and be 'cast out.'

The difference is very characteristic. As Lightfoot (p. 195) happily expresses it, 'the Christian Apostle and the philosophic Jew move in parallel lines, keeping side by side, and yet never once crossing each other's path.' Their allegorical explanations of the same history are 'most like and yet most unlike.' There is a similar relation of similitude and contrast between Philo's and St. John's doctrine of the divine Logos. It is the difference between a shadowy abstraction and a substantial reality. Philo sacrificed the obvious grammatical and historical sense to the spiritual and mystic; the Apostles never invalidate the historical sense. Philo put his Platonic ideas and fancies into the Old Testament; the Apostles drew out the deeper meaning of the same. Philo idealized the Mosaic religion till it evaporated into philosophical abstractions and mythical shadows; the Apostles spiritualized the Mosaic religion, and saw in it the type of the truth and reality of the gospel.

We add a few general remarks on typical and allegorical interpretation.

1. The sacred authors used language, like other writers, in order to be understood by the people whom they addressed. They intended one definite meaning, not two or three. This meaning can only be ascertained by grammatical and historical interpretation, according to the acknowledged laws of thought and speech, and in view of the conditions and surroundings of the author. This is the only sound and firm basis of all true exegesis.

2. The Bible has throughout a profound spiritual meaning, and admits of endless application. To find it, requires spiritual insight and sympathy, which is a greater and rarer gift than knowledge of grammar and critical acumen. But this spiritual meaning is *in* the letter, as the kernel is in the shell, and as the soul is in the body, not outside of, and contrary to, the plain, natural meaning of the words and phrases. Nor is it a second meaning besides the natural.

3. The whole Jewish dispensation, — including history, prophecy, worship, and ritual, — is a type and shadow of the Christian dispensation (Col. ii. 17; Hebr. viii. 5; ix. 23; x. 1). Every person, event, and institution expresses an actual idea or fact which is more fully expressed or developed by a corresponding idea or fact in the Christian dispensation. The typical significance depends on the connection with the central idea of the theocracy and the preparation for Christianity. The nearer a person or event to the person of Christ and the history of redemption, the deeper is their typical import. In a wider sense all history is typical and prophetical, and every period is a higher fulfilment of the preceding period. Hence 'there is nothing new under the sun;' and yet history never repeats itself. The New Testament is full of typical interpretation and application of the Old Testament; but there are no allegorical interpretations in the Gospels, and very few in the Epistles.

4. Allegorical interpretation, technically so called, as distinct from typical illustration and verification, assumes a double or threefold sense of the Scriptures, an obvious literal sense and a hidden spiritual or mystic sense, both of which were intended by the sacred writer. It was introduced into the Christian church by the learned Origen, who in this respect was more a disciple of Philo than of Paul, and distinguished three senses of the Bible, corresponding to the three constituent elements in man, — body, soul, and spirit. It extensively prevailed with various modifications in the Christian church, especially during the Middle Ages, and again in the seventeenth century. It opened the door to the most arbitrary treatment of the Bible and turned it into a nose of wax. It is irreverently reverent. It assumes that the plain natural sense of the Bible is not deep enough and must be improved by human ingenuity. It substitutes subjective fancies for objective truths, and pious imposition for honest exposition. It is not dead yet, and falsely appeals to St. Paul; forgetting that he was inspired, while we are not, and that he allegorized only two or three times, for illustration, rather than argument. Calvin, one of the soundest commentators, strongly protests against this abuse of Scripture, and says: 'As the Apostle declares that these things are allegorized, Origen and many others along with him, have seized the occasion of torturing Scripture, in every possible manner, away from the true sense. They concluded that the literal sense is too mean and poor. and that, under the outward bark of the letter, there lurk deeper mysteries which cannot be extracted but by beating out allegories And this they had no difficulty in accomplishing; for speculations which appear to be ingenious have always been preferred, and always will be preferred by the world to sound doctrine. For many centuries no man was considered to be ingenious, who had not the skill and daring necessary for changing into a variety of curious shapes the sacred word of God. This was undoubtedly a contrivance of Satan to undermine the authority of Scripture, and to take away from the reading of it the true benefit. God visited this profanation by a just judgment, when He suffered the pure meaning of the Scripture to be buried under false interpretations. I acknowledge that Scripture is a most rich and inexhaustible fountain of all wisdom; but I deny that its fertility consists in the various meanings which any

man, at his pleasure, may assign. Let us know, then, that the true meaning of Scripture is the natural and obvious meaning ; and let us embrace and abide by it resolutely.'

5. But even if we admit that Paul's typical allegory in this passage borders on the rabbinical exegesis of his age, from which, however, it differs very materially as we have shown, it cannot weaken our confidence in his inspiration. I quote the judicious remarks of Bishop Lightfoot (p. 197) : ' We need not fear to allow that St. Paul's mode of teaching here is colored by his early education in the rabbinical schools. It were as unreasonable to stake the Apostle's inspiration on the turn of a metaphor, or the character of an illustration, or the form of an argument, as on purity of diction. No one now thinks of maintaining that the language of the inspired writers reaches the classical standard of correctness and elegance, though at one time it was held almost a heresy to deny this. "A treasure contained in earthen vessels," "strength made perfect in weakness," "rudeness in speech, yet not in knowledge," such is the far nobler conception of inspired teaching, which we may gather from the Apostle's own language. And this language we should do well to keep in mind. But on the other hand it were sheer dogmatism to set up the intellectual standard of our own age or country as an infallible rule. The power of allegory has been differently felt in different ages, as it is differently felt at any one time by diverse nations. Analogy, allegory, metaphor — by what boundaries are these separated from each other ? What is true or false, correct or incorrect, as an analogy, or an allegory ? What argumentative force must be assigned to either ? We should, at least, be prepared with an answer to these questions, before we venture to sit in judgment on any individual case.'

CHAPTER V. .

Exhortation to Steadfastness in Christian Freedom, and Warning against Legal Bondage.

Chapter V. 1-12.

Here begins the practical part of the Epistle, consisting of exhortations and warnings appropriate to the occasion. First, the Apostle exhorts them to hold fast their spiritual freedom which they enjoy in Christ, and not to relapse again into legal bondage.

1 STAND fast therefore in *a* the liberty wherewith Christ hath
2 made us free,[1] and be not entangled again *b* with the [2] yoke of bondage. Behold, I Paul say unto you, that *c* if ye be cir-
3 cumcised, Christ shall[3] profit you nothing. For[4] I testify again to every man that is circumcised, *d* that he is a debtor to
4 do the whole law. *e* Christ is become of no effect unto you,[5] whosoever of you are justified by the law ;[6] *f* ye are fallen[7]
5 from grace. For we through the Spirit[8] *g* wait[9] for the hope
6 of righteousness by faith. For *h* in Jesus Christ[10] neither circumcision availeth any thing, nor uncircumcision ; but *i* faith
7 which worketh by love.[11] Ye *k* did run well ;[12] *l* who did hin-

a John viii. 32; Rom. vi. 18; 1 Pet. ii. 16.
b Acts xv. 10; ch. ii. 4; iv. 9.
c Acts xv. 1. See Acts xvi. 3.
d Ch. iii. 10.
e Rom. ix. 31, 32; ch. ii. 21.
f Heb. xii. 15
g Rom. viii. 24, 25; 2 Tim. iv. 8.
h 1 Cor. vii. 19; ch. iii. 28; vi. 15;
i 1 Thess. i. 3; Col. iii. 11. James ii. 18, 20, 22.
k 1 Cor. ix. 24.
l Ch. iii. 1.

1 for freedom did Christ make us free. *See notes.* 2 in a
3 will 4 Nay (*others*, Moreover)
5 Ye are cut off from Christ (*lit.* Ye were done away from Christ)
6 all ye who are being (*or* would be) justified by law 7 fallen away
8 by the Spirit from faith (*the words* from faith *are misplaced in the E. V. at the close of the verse*) 9 wait eagerly 10 Christ Jesus
11 faith working through love 12 Ye were running bravely

8 der you that ye should not obey the truth? This persuasion ^m ⁿ
9 *cometh* not of him ^m that calleth you. ⁿ A little leaven leaven-
10 eth the whole lump. ^o I have confidence in you through ¹³ the
Lord, that ye will be none otherwise minded : but ^p he that
troubleth you ^q shall bear his judgment, whosoever he be.
11 ^r And I, brethren, if I yet ¹⁴ preach circumcision, ^s why do I yet
suffer persecution ? ¹⁶ then is ^t the offence of the cross ceased. ¹⁶
12 ^u I would they were even cut off ^x which trouble you. ¹⁷

m Ch. i. 6.
n 1 Cor. v. 6;
xv. 33.
o 2 Cor. ii. 3.
viii. 22.
Chap. i. 7.
q 2 Cor. x. 6.
Chap. vi. 12.
s 1 Cor. xv. 30;
chap. iv. 29;
vi. 17.
t 1 Cor. i. 23.
u Josh. vii. 25;
1 Cor. v. 13;
chap. i. 8, 9.
x Acts xv. 1,
2, 24.

¹³ toward you in   ¹⁴ still   ¹⁵ am I still persecuted ?
¹⁶ hath . . . . been done away
¹⁷ I wish that they who are unsettling you would go beyond circumcision (go
on to abscission)

Ver. 1. **For freedom did Christ make (or set) us free: stand firm, therefore, and be not entangled again in a yoke of bondage.**[1] This exhortation is the inferential close of the argumentative, and a suitable beginning of the hortative, part of the Epistle. Some editors and commentators put the verse, either in whole or in part, at the end of chap. iv. Paul contrasts Christian freedom with Jewish bondage, and urges the Galatians to hold fast to the former, and not to relapse into the latter, or to exchange one form of slavery (their native heathenism) with another (Judaism). Hence ' again.' ' Freedom' is the outcome of the preceding discussion, and is emphatically put first. ' For,' or 'unto freedom' (better than ' *with* freedom,' although the Greek admits both), *i. e.*, in order that we might be and remain free. It is, of course, not carnal but spiritual freedom, freedom from the curse and bondage of the law, secured to the believer as a permanent condition by the vicarious death of Christ, which satisfied the demands of Divine justice and saved us from wrath. This freedom implies the consciousness of the full pardon of our sins, a ready and direct access to the throne of grace, and all the privileges and responsibilities of a son in his father's house. A Christian freeman is a grateful and cheerful servant of God, and a lord and king, though in chains, like Paul in Rome, who was a true freeman, while Nero on the throne was a miserable slave of his lusts. — ' Stand firm,' in this liberty of an evangelical Christian. — ' Yoke of bondage,' which bears down the neck and prevents free motion. Legalism is a burdensome slavery of the mind and conscience. Peter, in his speech at the Council of Jerusalem, likewise calls the law of Moses a ' yoke,' which ' neither our fathers nor we could bear,' Acts xv. 10. Luther remarks on this verse : ' Let us learn to count this our freedom most noble, exalted, and precious, which no emperor, no prophet, nor patriarch, no angel from heaven, but Christ, God's Son, hath obtained for us ; not for this that He might relieve us from a bodily and temporal subjection, but from a spiritual and eternal imprisonment of the cruelest tyrants, namely, the law, sin, death, devil.' Calvin : ' Paul reminds them that they ought not to despise a freedom so precious. And

certainly it is an invaluable blessing, in defence of which it is our duty to fight even to death. If men lay upon our shoulders an unjust burden, it may be borne ; but if they endeavor to bring our conscience into bondage, we must resist valiantly, even to death.'

Ver. 2. **Behold, I, Paul, say unto you, that if ye be circumcised** (suffer yourselves to be circumcised), **Christ will profit you nothing.** Your course is not only foolish, but dangerous, yea ruinous. A circumcised man may become a Christian, but a Christian who deliberately undergoes circumcision, becomes a Jew (a ' proselyte of righteousness ') and virtually trusts to the law for salvation, and not to Christ. ' Behold' rouses attention. ' I, Paul ' interposes the apostolic authority, in opposition to the Judaizing teachers who taught that circumcision was necessary to make them full Christians and to insure salvation. ' If ye be circumcised,' or ' submit to circumcision,' as a term of salvation ; some had probably done so already. ' Christ will profit you nothing ; ' the future marks the certain result of this Judaizing course. Luther : ' If St. Paul can venture to pass so terrible a judgment against the law and circumcision which God himself has given, what kind of judgment would he utter upon the chaff and the dross of men's ordinances ? Wherefore this text is such a thunder-clap, that by right the whole papal realm should be astounded and terrified.'

Ver. 3. **Nay, I testify again to every man that is circumcised** (suffers himself to be circumcised), **that he is a debtor to do the whole law.** Circumcision is an initiatory rite by which the person circumcised becomes a Jew, and assumes the solemn obligation to keep the whole law of Moses, moral and ritual ; just as the baptismal vow is a pledge of obedience to the gospel of Christ. The sacramental rite implies all the responsibilities and duties as well as privileges of membership. ' I testify,' I bear witness, I solemnly assert as in court. (In classical Greek the verb usually means to summon as a witness, to call to witness.) ' Again ' refers to ' I say ' in ver. 2. ' To every man,' without exception, stronger than the preceding general ' ye.'

Ver. 4. **Ye are cut off from Christ all ye who are being** (or, would be) **justified by (the) law ;** which (or, for which) Christ made us free, and be not,' etc (τῇ ἐλευθερίᾳ οὖν, ᾗ Χριστὸς ἡμᾶς ἠλευθέρωσεν, στήκετε). But the oldest MSS. (א B, etc.) put ' therefore ' (οὖν) after ' stand ' (στήκετε), and omit ' with which '(ᾗ). The punctuation is a matter of interpretation.

---

[1] This is upon the whole the best reading (adopted by Bengel, Lachmann, Tischendorf, ed. viii., Meyer). The MSS. and versions vary considerably, although the sense is not essentially altered. The received text reads literally: ' Stand firm therefore in (or, in respect to) the freedom with

ye are fallen away from grace. 'Ye are cut off from Christ,' completely separated from Him. The Greek verb means to be annulled, to be done away with. Your union with Christ was dissolved and came to nothing in the moment when you sought your justification in the law. 'Ye are fallen away from grace,' not totally and finally (in which case the warning would be useless), but for the time being. Looking to God's promise and faithfulness, our salvation is sure ; looking to our weakness and temptations, all is doubtful, unless we watch and pray without ceasing.

Ver. 5. For we, by the Spirit, from faith wait eagerly for the hope of righteousness. 'For' introduces an argument from the opposite for the judgment passed in ver. 4 against those who seek justification by the law. 'By the Spirit,' the Holy Spirit, who is the Divine source of faith and spiritual life in us. 'From faith,' which is the subjective source of our expectation. 'Wait eagerly,' or persistently, patiently. The hope of the Christian does not decline, but increase until the time of fruition. Comp. Rom. viii. 19, 23, 25 ; 1 Cor. i. 7 ; Phil. iii. 20. 'For the hope of righteousness,' the righteousness hoped for by us as a possession that is secured here by faith, but extends into eternity and involves the bliss and glory of the future life. Comp. Rom. viii. 30. Others take 'hope' as equivalent to the crown of glory which awaits the justified as their reward. The passage affords no aid to the doctrine of a gradual increase of justification, which, as Meyer says here, 'is entirely un-Pauline. Justification does not, like sanctification, unfold itself and increase, but it has as its normal consequence sanctification through the Spirit, which is given to him who is justified by faith. Thus Christ is to us righteousness and sanctification. 1 Cor. i. 30.'

Ver. 6. For in Christ Jesus neither circumcision availeth anything, nor uncircumcision; but faith working (or operative) through love. A most important passage both doctrinally and practically, a remedy against sectarianism, and a key for the solution of many bitter controversies in the history of the Church. Paul positively condemned circumcision as a term of justification and salvation ; now he qualifies the condemnation, viewing circumcision as a mere outward form and accidental distinction. A Jewish Christian and a Gentile Christian are equal before God ; the circumcision of the one is no advantage, and the uncircumcision of the other is no disadvantage : all depends upon their union with Christ. Comp. Gal. vi. 15 ; 1 Cor. vii. 18-20. 'For in Christ Jesus neither circumcision availeth anything, nor uncircumcision.' May we not add in the very spirit of Paul ? ' neither episcopacy nor presbytery, neither presbytery nor independency, neither immersion nor sprinkling, neither Calvinism nor Arminianism, neither Catholicism nor Protestantism, nor any other isms, however important in their place, are of any account, when compared with the fundamental difference between faith and infidelity, between Christ and anti-Christ. Heaven will embrace members of all creeds and sects, and the sole condition of entrance will be 'faith working through love.' The Greek verb (ἐνεργοῦμαι) here translated ' working,' or ' operative,' has in the

New Testament always the middle sense (comp. Rom. viii. 5; 2 Cor. i. 6; Col. i. 29; 1 Thess. ii. 13; James v. 16). The passive rendering : 'wrought' or 'made energetic through love,' must be abandoned.[1] Paul unites here the three cardinal virtues, faith, hope (ver. 5), and love. In this triad of Christian graces ' consists the whole of Christianity' (Bengel).

The sentence, 'faith working through love,' reconciles the doctrine of Paul with that of James.[2] Comp. vi. 15 ; 1 Thess. i. 3 ; 1 Cor. xiii. ; 1 Tim. i. 5; James ii. 22. Here is the basis for a final settlement of the controversy on the doctrine of justification. Romanism (following exclusively the language of James) teaches justification by faith and works; Protestantism (on the authority of Paul) : justification by faith alone ; St. Paul and St. James combined : justification and salvation by faith working through love. Man is justified by faith alone, but faith remains not alone, it is the fruitful mother of good works, which are summed up in love to God and love to men. Faith and love are as inseparable as light and heat in the sun. Christ's merits are the objective and meritorious ground of justification, faith (as the organ of appropriation) is the subjective condition, love or good works are the necessary evidence ; without love faith is dead, according to James, or no faith at all, according to Paul. A great deal of misunderstanding in this and other theological controversies has arisen from the different use of terms.

Ver 7. Ye were running bravely. The martial and heroic spirit of Paul often compares the course of Christian life with the running of a race in the stadium. Comp. ii. 2 ; Phil. iii. 14 ; 1 Cor. ix. 24-27 ; 2 Tim. iv. 7.

Ver. 8. Of him that calleth you, God ; comp. note on i. 6 ; and Phil. iii.13, 'the prize of the high calling of God in Christ Jesus.' The Father draws to the Son by the Spirit through the gospel.

Ver. 9. A little leaven leaveneth the whole lump. A proverbial expression for the all-pervading influence of a good or bad principle. Here used in a bad sense, as 1 Cor. v. 6 and Mark viii. 15, and often by rabbinical writers. The Judaizing doctrine of the necessity of circumcision poisons the whole system of Christian doctrine and practice. Others less aptly apply it to the persons of the false teachers who corrupt the mass of the people. In a good sense the figure of the leaven is used of the kingdom of heaven which penetrates all the faculties and powers of man and of society. Matt. xiii. 32 ; Luke xiii. 21.

Ver. 10. I have confidence toward (or in regard to) you in the Lord, etc. Paul hopes that the Galatians will return from their error, and this hope is grounded in his communion with Christ in whom he lived and moved. Comp. Phil. ii. 24 ; 2 Thess. iii. 4 ; Rom. xiv. 14.— He that troubleth you, all the false teachers. Comp. ver. 12 ; 2 Cor. xi. 4.— Shall bear his judgment, God's judgment of condemnation. Comp. Rom. ii. 3 ; xiii. 2 ; 1 Cor. xi. 29. The guilty must 'bear' the sentence as a burden.— Whosoever he be, whatever be his character and position (Jerome thinks even of Peter, but without any good reason; for Peter agreed with Paul in principle and failed only in practice at Antioch.)

---

[1] Advocated by some of the fathers and Roman Catholic commentators in support of the doctrine of ' fides caritate formata,' for which the passage is quoted by the Council of Trent in the decree on justification (Sess. vi., ch. 7). Windischmann, a modern R. C. commentator on Galatians, gives up the passive meaning, but still clings to the Tridentine use of the passage against the Protestant doctrine of justification by faith only

[2] Lightfoot: ' These words bridge the gulf which seems to separate the language of St. Paul and St. James. Both assert a principle of practical energy, as opposed to a barren, inactive theory.'

Ver. 11. If I still preach circumcision, why am I still persecuted? Then hath the offence (or stumbling block) of the cross been done away. The first 'still' refers to the time since his conversion from Judaism. If circumcision is preached as a condition of salvation, then the cross, that is, the crucifixion, the doctrine of salvation by the atoning death of Christ, has lost its offensive character to the Jews, and there is no further reason for persecution by the Jews. The false teachers had probably spread the malicious report that Paul himself preached circumcision, because he practised it in the case of Timothy who had a Jewish mother (Acts xvi. 1-3); but this was exceptional and a measure of expediency and charity, not a surrender of the principle.

Ver. 12. I wish that they who are unsettling you would even go on to abscission; that the circumcisers would not stop with the half measure of circumcision. but go beyond it even to abscission or mutilation (make themselves eunuchs), like the priests of Cybele. A severe irony similar to the one in Phil. iii. 2, 3, where Paul calls the

boasters of 'circumcision' the 'concision.' Self-mutilation was a recognized form of heathen worship, especially in Pessinus in Galatia, and therefore quite familiar to the readers. Thus by glorying in the flesh the Galatians relapsed into their former heathenism. The words may be explained: 'cut themselves off' from your communion, but the interpretation above given agrees best with the meaning of the verb, and the 'even' (which points to something more than circumcision), and is maintained by the Greek fathers and the best modern commentators. The translation of the E. V. 'were even cut off,' i. e., excommunicated, is ungrammatical (the Greek verb is in the middle, not the passive mood), and due to false delicacy. Christianity has abolished the revolting practice of self-mutilation, so that even the word is offensive; but in the days of Paul it was still in full force in Galatia, and is continued among Mohammedans who employ many eunuchs (especially in harems). Paul had evidently the dangerous power of sarcasm, but he used it very sparingly, and only in a worthy cause.

Warning against the Abuse of Freedom, and Exhortation to Brotherly Love.

CHAPTER V. 13-15.

In the spirit of true Christian wisdom and moderation, the Apostle now warns the readers against the danger of abusing Christian freedom and running it into antinomian license. This passage is chiefly directed to those Galatians who remained faithful to the free gospel as preached by Paul, but were exposed to the danger of running into the opposite extreme of lawlessness.

13 FOR, brethren, ye have been called unto liberty;[1] only [a]*use* not liberty for an occasion to the flesh,[2] but [b]by
14 love serve one another. For [c]all the law[3] is fulfilled in one word, *even* in this: [d]'Thou shalt love thy neighbor as thyself,'
15 But if ye bite and devour one another, take heed that ye be not consumed one of another.

[a] 1 Cor. viii 9; 1 Pet. ii. 16.
[b] 1 Cor. ix 19; chap. vi. 2.
[c] Matt. vii. 12; xxii. 40; James ii. 8
[d] Lev. xix 18; Matt. xxii. 39; Rom. 8, 9.

[1] For ye were called unto freedom, brethren
[2] *turn* not your freedom into an occasion for the flesh
[3] the entire law

Ver. 13. For ye were called unto freedom, brethren. The word 'for' justifies the indignant scorn of the preceding verse. 'Unto' denotes the object of the Christian calling. — Only (turn) not your freedom into an occasion (or, opportunity) for the flesh. A sudden check: freedom, but not license. True freedom is self-government and inseparable from law; it is a law to itself. How often has the word freedom been abused and perverted into its diabolical caricature! So also the truly Christian ideas of equality and fraternity. Gentile churches, like that of Corinth, were especially liable to the abuse of freedom and sensual excesses. The verb *turn* or *make* or *use* must be supplied (as often in animated passages of the classical writers). 'An occasion,' a starting-point, an opportunity (comp. Rom. vii. 8, 11; 2 Cor. v.

12; xi. 12; 1 Tim. v. 14). — But by love serve one another. By faith we are lords, by love we are servants of all. Show your freedom by love, and your love by service. This kind of bondage is honorable and delightful. 'To serve God is true freedom' (Augustin).

Ver. 14. For the entire law is (hath been and is) fulfilled in one word (even), in this: Thou shalt love thy neighbor as thyself. The law commands supreme love to God (in the first table), and love to our neighbor as to ourselves (in the second table). Love to our neighbor springs necessarily from love to God, and is impossible without it. The teaching of Christ (Matt. xxii. 39) and of the Apostle (comp. Rom. xiii. 8, 9) here perfectly agree. 'The neighbor.' In the Hebrew law, Levit. xix. 18, probably restricted to the

Jewish people, but by Christ extended to the universal brotherhood of men. Comp. Matt. v. 43, and the parable of the good Samaritan, Luke x. 29.

Ver. 15. **But if ye bite and devour one another,** like wild beasts. How applicable this to all sectarian and partisan strifes which turn the church into a battle-field and impair its force against the common enemy!

Walking by the Spirit. The Works of the Flesh and the Fruit of the Spirit.

CHAPTER V. 16-25.

Paul exhorts the Galatians to lead a truly Christian life under the guidance of the Holy Spirit, and contrasts the vices of the flesh with the graces of the Spirit. Such exhortations and contrasts are impossible on heathen soil, or in the sphere of natural morality, and reveal the lofty spirituality of the Christian religion.

16 *THIS* I say then,[1] *a* Walk in[2] the Spirit, and ye shall not[3]
17 fulfil the lust of the flesh. For *b* the flesh lusteth against the Spirit, and the Spirit against the flesh : and[4] these are contrary[5] the one to the other ; *c* so that ye cannot[6] do the
18 things that ye would. But *d* if ye be[7] led of the Spirit, *e* ye are
19 not under the law. Now *f* the works of the flesh are manifest, which are *these*,[8] Adultery,[9] fornication, uncleanness, lascivious-
20 ness, Idolatry, witchcraft,[10] hatred,[11] variance,[12] emulations,[13]
21 wrath,[14] strife,[15] seditions,[16] heresies,[17] Envyings, murders,[18] drunkenness, revellings, and such like : of the[19] which I tell you before,[20] as I have also told *you* in time past,[21] that *g* they which[22] do such things shall not inherit the kingdom of God.
22 But *h* the fruit of the Spirit is love, joy, peace, longsuffering,
23 *i* gentleness,[23] *k* goodness, *l* faith,[24] Meekness, temperance :[25]
24 *m* against such there is no law. And[26] they that are Christ's[27] *n* have crucified[28] the flesh with the[29] affections[30] and lusts.
25 *o* If we live in[31] the Spirit, let us also walk in[31] the Spirit.
26 *p* Let us not be desirous of vainglory,[32] provoking one another, envying one another.

a Rom. vi. 12; viii. 1, 4, 13; xiii. 14;
vers. 25; 1 Pet. ii. 11.
b Rom. vii. 23; viii. 6, 7
c Rom. vii. 15, 18, 19.
d Rom. viii. 14
e Rom. vi. 14.
f 1 Cor. iii. 3; 2 Cor. xii. 21; Eph. v. 3; Col. iii. 5; James iii. 14, 15;
Mark vii. 22.
g 1 Cor. vi. 9 Eph. v. 5; Col. iii. 6; Rev. xxii. 15.
h John xv. 2 ; Eph. v. 9. Col. iii. 12; James iii. 17.
k Rom. xv. 14. *l* 1 Cor. xiii 7;
m 1 Tim. i. 9.
n Rom. vi. 6; xiii. 14; chap. ii. 20;
1 Pet. ii. 11.
o Rom. viii. 4, 5; vers 16.
p Phil. ii. 3.

[1] Now I say   [2] by   [3] in no wise   [4] for   [5] opposed
[6] other, that ye may not   [7] are   [8] of which kind are
[9] *omit* adultery (*according to the best authorities*)   [10] sorcery
[11] hatreds (*or* enmities)   [12] strife   [13] rivalry
[14] outbursts of wrath   [15] factions   [16] divisions   [17] parties
[18] *omit* murders (*according to* ℵ *and B.*)   [19] *omit* the
[20] I forewarn you   [21] as I did tell you before   [22] who
[23] benignity   [24] faithfulness   [25] self-control   [26] Now
[27] of Christ Jesus   [28] did crucify   [29] its   [30] passions
[31] by   [32] become vainglorious

Ver. 16. Paul returns to the warning in ver. 13, not to abuse the freedom for an occasion to the flesh. — **Walk by the Spirit,** according to the rule and direction of the Holy Spirit who is the higher conscience and controlling principle of the Christian. Comp. iv. 6; Rom. viii. 2. — **And** ye shall in no wise fulfil the lust of the flesh. The Holy Spirit and the sinful flesh are so antagonistic and irreconcilable that to follow the one is to resist and defeat the other. The 'flesh' is here, as in vers. 13, 17, 19, and often in Paul (also John iii. 6), used in a moral sense, and designates the fallen, carnal, sinful nature of man. It is not confined to sensuality, but embraces also the evil dispositions of the mind (ver. 20). It must not be confounded with 'body;' it uses and abuses the body as its organ, but the body is good in itself, nd intended to become the organ of the regenerate spirit of man and the temple of the Holy Spirit of God. 1 Cor. vi. 19, 20; comp. iii. 16; 2 Cor. vi. 16. (Comp. Excursus on Rom. vii., and the elaborate discussion of Wieseler on Gal. iii. 13, pp. 442-455.) The antagonism between the carnal nature of man and the Holy Spirit of God is one of the fundamental ideas in Paul's psychology. The Gnostics and Manichæans carried it to the extreme of dualism between mind and matter; but this is a heretical perversion. Paul's antagonism is *moral*, not physical, and rests on the recognition of the body as substantially good and redeemable by the same power of God. which redeems the soul.

Ver. 17. For the flesh lusteth against the Spirit, and the Spirit (*strives*) against the flesh. There is a conflict between reason and appetite, between conscience and depravity, between the higher and lower aspirations, between heaven and hell, going on in every man who is roused to a sense of duty and responsibility; but this conflict becomes most serious under the awakening influence of the Holy Spirit (who is meant here), and results in the triumph of one principle and the defeat of the other. Comp. Rom. vii. 4 ff. 'The strife of the Spirit against the flesh is an infallible token of regeneration and a state of grace, and is distinguished from the strife of the mere powers of reason in this that the former always wins the victory' (Starke). 'The state of the believer is conflict, but with final victory' (Ellicott.) The natural man may acquire a Stoic virtue, and achieve a conquest over his lower appetites, but not over his pride, which rises all the more powerful on the ruin of vulgar passions.

Ver. 18. But if ye are led by the Spirit, ye are not under (the) law. Comp. Rom. viii. 14: 'As many as are led by the Spirit of God, they are the sons of God.' The Spirit 'leads' and guides men as moral and responsible beings, but does not drive or force them; hence it is possible to resist and to quench the Spirit (1 Thess. v. 19), to grieve Him (Eph. iv. 30), and even to blaspheme Him and thus to commit the unpardonable sin (Matt. xii. 32). Paul's conversion was sudden and radical, but not forced; he might have 'kicked against the goads' (Acts xxvi. 14), although it was 'hard' (not impossible) for Him to do so. 'Ye are not under the law,' under the dominion of the law which threatens death and keeps the conscience in constant terror. The law is a restraint of the flesh; to be free from the flesh is to be free from the restraint and curse of the law. The Spirit leads us into the fulfilment of the law of love (ver. 14), and the law ceases to be a yoke for trembling slaves, and becomes a rule for loving and grateful children and freemen. Luther: 'So great is the power and dominion of the Spirit that the law cannot accuse the godly. For Christ is our righteousness whom we apprehend by faith. He is without sin, and therefore the law cannot accuse

Him. As long as we cleave fast unto Him, we are led by the Spirit and are free from the law.'

Vers. 19-21. Now the works of the flesh are manifest, of which kind (or such as) are. The practical test of the fruits by which a tree is known (comp. Matt. vii. 16). 'Manifest,' plain and obvious to everybody. Paul does not aim at a complete and systematic catalogue of sins, but singles out those to which the Galatians from former habits and surroundings were specially exposed. He mentions (1) sins of sensuality or sins against *ourselves*: adultery [omitted in the best MSS.], fornication, uncleanness, lasciviousness (comp. 2 Cor. xii. 21); these were so common among all the heathen that no ancient moralist, not even Socrates, or Plato, or Cicero, absolutely condemned them (except adultery, because it interferes with the rights of a husband), and that they were even sanctioned by religion and connected with the worship of Venus or Aphrodite. The difference between Christian and heathen morality in this respect is like the difference between day and night. Paul condemns fornication as a prostitution and desecration of the temple of the Holy Spirit (1 Cor. vi. 15-20; iii. 16). (2) Spiritual sins against *God*, which are likewise characteristic of heathenism: idolatry, the worship of false gods (and all idolatrous practices), and sorcery, or magic, 'a secret tampering with the powers of evil,' usually associated with open idolatry (comp. Acts xix. 19; Rev. xxi. 8). (3) Sins against our *neighbor*, or various violations of brotherly love in feeling and action: hatreds (or enmities), strife, rivalry (or emulation), outbursts of wrath, factions, divisions (not seditions), parties (not heresies, in the later doctrinal sense), envyings, murders (comp. 2 Cor. xii. 20; Rom. i. 29). 'Murders' is omitted by the best MSS. (4) Sins of intemperance, very common among the Celtic nations: drunkenness, revellings, and such like (comp. Rom. xiii. 13; 1 Pet. iv. 3).

Ver. 21. Of which I forewarn you, as I did tell you before, on my former visits (i. 9; iv. 13, 16), when I preached to you the gospel which is death to all forms of immorality, and demands conformity to the holy character of Christ. They who do such things shall not inherit the kingdom of God, unless they be converted and sanctified. A hard and terrible word, yet most true (comp. 1 Cor. vi. 9, 10; xv. 50; Rev. xxii. 15). Heaven is the abode of absolute purity, and nothing unclean can enter therein. 'Without sanctification no man shall see the Lord.' Heb. xii. 14.

Vers. 22, 23. But the fruit of the Spirit is love, joy, peace, longsuffering, benignity, goodness, faithfulness, meekness, temperance. A string of pearls. One 'fruit,' in distinction of the many 'works of the flesh,' indicates the unity of the spiritual graces which are comprehended in love (ver. 14; comp. Eph. v. 9 'the fruit of the light,' and v. 11 'the unfruitful works of darkness).' 'The fruit is produced by the grace of God; the works of the flesh spring from ourselves' (Chrysostom). The list differs widely from pagan catalogues of virtues which have no place for love, humility, and meekness, joy and peace, nor any of the more delicate graces of the Spirit of God. There are four groups: (1.) 'Love,' the fundamental Christian grace which comprehends all others and 'holds heaven and earth in its embrace.' (2.) 'Joy' and 'peace,' the fundamental state of the Christian, his inward happiness, cheerfulness, and tranquillity which results from the remission of sin, the reconciliation to God, and the prospect of heaven. No one can be truly happy in this world who is not sure of eternal happiness in the world to come. (3.) 'Longsuffering,' 'benignity,' 'goodness,' 'faithfulness' (or fidelity), 'meekness,' are various forms of unselfish charity towards our fellow-men. 'Longsuffering' denotes patient endurance under injuries ; 'benignity,' kindly disposition ; 'goodness,' active benevolence ; 'faithfulness' (not 'faith' towards God), is here fidelity, trustfulness in our dealings with others ('love believeth all things,' 1 Cor. xiii. 7), in opposition to suspicion and distrust; 'meekness' (or gentleness), a mild and patient temper which bears and overcomes injuries (comp. Matt. v. 5 ; Ps. xxxvii. 11). (4.) 'Self-control' (temperance) refers to our conduct towards ourselves, and embraces moral self-government and moderation in all things, in opposition to carnal self-indulgence and intemperance in eating and drinking (comp. Acts xxiv. 25; 1 Cor. vii. 9). Luther : 'Jerome expounds this of virginity only, as though they that are married could not be chaste ; or as though the Apostle did write these things only to virgins. In the first and second chapter to Titus, he warns all bishops, young women, and married folks, both man and wife, to be chaste and pure.'—**Against such** (things) **there is no law** (of restraint). The law forbids and restrains sin and vice, but not the works of the Spirit, on the contrary it enjoins them ; comp. ver. 18, 'If ye are led by the Spirit, ye are not under (the restraining and condemning power of) the law ;' and 1 Tim. i. 9, 'Law is not made for a righteous man, but for the lawless and unruly, for the ungodly and sinners.' False interpretations : 'Such *persons* the law does not condemn ;' or 'Such *persons* need no law.' The Greek word for 'such' is neuter, and refers to the preceding virtues; as 'such like,' ver. 21, refers to the preceding vices.

Ver. 24. **Now they that are of Christ Jesus did crucify the flesh with its passions and lusts.** Union with Christ is a complete separation from

sin; hence the baptismal formula of renunciation of the flesh, the world, and the devil, and devotion to the service of Christ. Conversion is death of the old man and birth of the new. 'Passions' are passive, 'lusts' active, vices. The destruction of the old man of sin is an imitation of the crucifixion, as the birth of the new man of righteousness corresponds to the resurrection of Christ (comp. ii. 20; vi. 14; Rom. vi. 4-6; Col. iii. 5). The Greek aorist represents this ethical and subjective crucifixion as an act accomplished in the past at the time of conversion and baptism (comp. iii. 27); but in the nature of the case it is continued from day to day, as long as sin and temptation remain.

Ver. 25. **If we live by the Spirit, let us also walk by the Spirit.** Application to the Galatians, Paul included. To live and to walk are related here as condition and action, or as the inward and the outward life. If we live in the higher element of the Holy Spirit, we must also show it by a corresponding conduct (comp. ver. 16; Rom. viii. 5, 6). The dative in Greek here denotes the rule or direction (as vi. 16). 'By,' in English, has both the instrumental and the normal force.

Ver. 26. **Let us not become vainglorious,** etc. This is the opposite of humility (Phil. ii. 3). 'St. Paul works round again to the subject of ver. 15, and repeats his warning. It is clear that something had occurred which alarmed him on this point' (Lightfoot). Vanity and quarrelsomeness, self-exaltation, and self-seeking were among the darling sins of the Gauls. But as Luther says, 'love of vainglory is a common vice all the world over in all conditions. In the smallest village there are some peasants who deem themselves wiser and better than the rest, and like to be looked up to. But nowhere is this vice so harmful as in the officers of the church.' Calvin remarks : 'It is not lawful for us to glory but in God alone. Every other kind of glorying is pure vanity. Mutual provocations and envyings are the daughters of ambition.' Ver. 26 is the connecting link between ch. v. and ch. vi.

CHAPTER VI.

I. Miscellaneous Exhortations, vers. 1-10.   II. Autograph Warning against the Judaizers, vers. 11-17.   III. Concluding Benediction, ver. 18.

Miscellaneous Exhortations.

Chapter VI. 1-10.

The Apostle exhorts the Galatians to deal gently with a weak brother, to bear the brother's burden, to be on their guard against conceit, to be liberal to their teachers, and to persevere in doing good.

1 BRETHREN,[1] *a* if a man be overtaken in a fault,[2] ye *b* which [3] are spiritual, restore such a one *c* in the spirit of meek-

2 ness; considering [4] thyself, *d* lest thou also be tempted. *e* Bear

a Rom. xiv. 1; xv. 1; Heb. xii. 13; James v. 19.
b 1 Cor. ii. 15; iii. 1.
c 1 Cor iv. 21; 2 Thess. iii. 15; 2 Tim. ii. 25.
d 1 Cor. vii. 5; x. 12.
e Rom. xv. 1; chap. v. 13; 1 Thess. v. 14.

[1] even   [2] in (*or* by) any transgression   *8* who
[4] looking (*each one individually*) to

3 ye one another's burdens, and so fulfil [5] [f] the law of Christ.   For [f] John xiii.
    [g] if a man think himself to be something, when [h] he is nothing,[6]
4 he deceiveth himself.   But [i] let every [7] man prove his own
    work, and then shall he have rejoicing in himself alone, and [g]
5 [k] not in another.[8]   For [l] every [9] man shall bear his own bur-
6 den.   [m] Let [10] him that is taught in the word communicate [11]
    unto him that teacheth in all good things.
7   [n] Be not deceived; [o] God is not mocked : for [p] whatsoever a
8 man soweth, that shall he also reap.   [q] For he that soweth to
    his [12] flesh shall of [13] the flesh reap corruption ; but he that sow-
    eth to [14] the Spirit shall of [15] the Spirit reap life everlasting.[16]
9 And [17] [r] let us not be weary in well doing : for in due season
10 we shall reap, [s] if we faint not.   [t] As we have therefore [18] op-
    portunity, [u] let us do good unto all *men*,[19] especially unto them
    who are [20] of [v] the household of faith.

[5] ye shall fulfil (*according to another reading*)   [6] being nothing   [7] each
[8] his ground for boasting (*or glorying*) in regard to himself alone, and not
another (*or*, his neighbor)   [9] each   [10] But let
[11] impart (*lit.*, go shares with)   [12] unto his own   [18] from
[14] unto   [15] from   [16] eternal   [17] But
[18] So then as (*or while*) we have   [19] *omit men*   [20] to the members

Rev. ii. 10.   [t] John ix. 4; xii. 35.   [u] 1 Thess. v. 15; 1 Tim. vi. 18; Tit. iii. 8.   [v] Eph. ii. 19; Heb. iii. 6.

Right margin references:
[f] John xiii. 14, 15; 34;
xv. 12;
James ii. 8;
1 John iv. 21.
[g] Rom. xii. 3; 1 Cor. viii.
2; chap. ii. 6.
[h] 2 Cor. iii. 5; xii. 11.
[i] 1 Cor. xi. 28; 2 Cor. xiii. 5.
[k] See Luke xviii. 11.
[l] Rom. ii. 6; 1 Cor. iii. 8.
[m] Rom. xv. 27; 1 Cor. ix. 11, 14.
[n] 1 Cor. vi. 9; xv. 33.
[o] Job xiii. 9.
[p] Luke xvi. 25; Rom. ii. 6; 2 Cor. ix. 6.
[q] Job iv. 8; Prov. xi. 18; xxii. 8;
Hos. viii. 7; x. 12; Rom. viii. 13;
James iii. 18.
[r] 1 Cor. xv. 58; 2 Thess. iii. 13.
[s] Matt. xxiv. 13; Heb. iii. 6, 14; x. 36; xii. 3, 5;

Ver. 1. Spiritual life (v. 25, 26) must show itself in spiritual action, especially in charity, meekness, and modesty. — **Brethren.** A word of love more potent than argument. — **Even if a man be overtaken** or surprised, before he is aware of it or able to resist. Sins of precipitancy. We ought to take this charitable view of our neighbor's trespasses as far as possible. If ' even ' be connected with the verb (caught in the very act), an aggravation of the offence would be implied, but this is not consistent with the context. — **Ye that are spiritual,** or ' Ye the spiritual ones,' who are possessed and animated by the Holy Spirit. This refers back to chap. v. 25, and especially to that part of the congregation which remained faithful to the teaching of Paul. Comp. ' Ye are strong,' Rom. xv. 1. True charity is a test of spirituality. True strength and freedom show themselves in bearing and forbearing. — **In the spirit of meekness,** stronger than ' in a meek spirit.' Comp. 1 Cor. iv. 21, 'in love and a spirit of meekness.' — **Looking to thyself,** taking heed each one of you. An individualizing transition from the plural to the singular which makes the charge more direct.

Ver. 2. **Bear ye one another's burdens,** all sorts of troubles, cares, errors, and infirmities. Sin and error should be resisted and rebuked in a spirit of charity and meekness ; but with all our faults we ought to esteem and love one another as brethren in Christ. (Comp. Rom. xv. 1.) — **And thus ye shall** (completely) **fulfil the law of Christ,** namely, the law of love. (Comp. v. 14; Rom. xiii. 8 ; John xiii. 34 ; 1 John iii. 23.) The E. V. is based on another reading which expresses the imperative, instead of the future. The authorities are almost equally divided.

Ver. 3. The best motive of forbearance towards others is the sense of our own weakness. — **Being nothing,** notwithstanding his conceit. Every man is apt to overestimate himself ; humility is one of the rarest, but sweetest graces. ' In Christian morality self-esteem is vanity, and vanity is nothingness.'

Ver. 4. If a man desires to find cause for boasting, let him test and examine his own actions, and not contrast his fancied virtues with the faults of his neighbor. But every sincere self-examination results in humiliation. — **His own work,** collective and emphatic : the aggregate of his actions.

Ver. 5. **For each man shall bear his own burden.** No contradiction to ver. 2. Those who bear their own burden are best able to sympathize with others and to share in their burdens. Those who pray most for themselves pray most for others. ' Each is to prove his own work and not to leave it to be accomplished by others, and at the same time each is to help all others as often as he can find opportunity. And the opportunity to bless others is itself one of the greatest of blessings.' Paul is fond of paradoxes and antithetic expressions of complementary truths (comp. Phil. ii. 12, 13 ; 2 Cor. xii. 10 ; ' when I am weak, then I am strong ').

Ver. 6. **Let him that is taught** (or, orally instructed) **in the word** (of God) **share with him that teacheth, in all good things** (temporal possessions of every kind). Injunction of the duty of the congregation to support liberally their teachers. Their relation is a partnership, a communion of interests. They are mutually dependent and helpful, and should share each other's blessings and burdens. Temporal support is but a small return for spiritual blessings. The Gala-tians needed this exhortation very much. They were asked to contribute to the suffering churches in Judæa (1 Cor. xvi. 1), but we do not learn that they did it. The niggardly spirit of the Gauls was proverbial.[1] Paul set a noble example of self-denial in supporting himself as a tent-maker, preaching the gospel by day and working at his trade by night! Only by exception he received contributions from his beloved Philippians. And he was never weary to take up collections in his poor congregations for the support of the still poorer brethren in Judæa. But as our Saviour laid down the principle 'that the laborer is worthy of his hire' (Luke x. 7), so the Apostle repeatedly urges upon his readers the duty of supporting their teachers. See 1 Thess. ii. 6, 9 ; 1 Cor. ix. 4 ff. ; 2 Cor. xi. 7 ff. ; Phil. iv. 10 ff. ; 1 Tim. v. 17, 18. The less a minister says on the pulpit about his salary the better ; but sometimes duty requires plain talk on this delicate subject. The passage implies that the church ought to be supported by voluntary contributions of the people, not by taxation, which checks the exercise of liberality, and is apt to create indifference and dislike.

Ver. 7. Enforces the duty of liberality. It carries in itself its own exceeding great reward, for 'it is more blessed to give than to receive,' and sows the seed for a rich harvest in heaven ; while illiberality and stinginess belittles and beggars the man here, and lets him go empty on the great day of reward. — **Be not deceived.** How many deceive themselves and imagine that they can withhold from their minister his just dues without incurring the displeasure of God. — **God is not mocked,** cannot be treated with contempt without provoking his righteous punishment. — **Whatsoever a man soweth, that shall he also reap.** (Comp. 2 Cor. ix. 6.) A proverbial expression (Job iv. 8), found also among classical writers (Aristotle, Cicero, etc.), but here spiritualized and applied to the

[1] Livy calls the Galatians 'avidissima rapiendi gens' (xxxviii. 27).

future reward and punishment. The present life is the seed time, the future life the harvest. Who sows grain will reap grain, who sows tares will reap tares ; who sows plentifully will reap plentifully, who sows sparingly will reap sparingly. Those who keep this great truth constantly before their eyes will redeem every hour and use every opportunity to do good.

Ver. 8. **He that soweth unto (upon) his own flesh shall from the flesh reap corruption ; but he that soweth unto (upon) the Spirit shall from the Spirit reap life eternal.** Ver. 7 speaks of the kind of seed sown ('whatsoever'), ver. 8 of the kind of soil on which the seed is sown. The soil of the flesh, that is of corrupt human nature, yields blighted and rotten fruit ; the soil of the Holy Spirit yields sweet and healthy fruit, even eternal happiness and peace.

Ver. 9. **But let us not be weary** (lose heart) **in well doing.** Not only in regard to the duty of liberality, but in every good work. (Comp. 2 Thess. iii. 13.) 'Fatigue is not weariness. In well-doing we are more apt to be weary than fatigued' (Riddle). — **In due season we shall reap,** in the time of harvest (comp. 1 Tim. ii. 6 ; vi. 15 ; Tit. i. 3). 'The due season is God's season' (Riddle). **If we faint not,** 'as husbandmen overcome with heat and fatigue.' (Comp. James v. 7.)

Ver. 10. **So then as we have opportunity** (lit., a seasonable time). Each opportunity for doing good is an angel that offers us his services. If neglected, it may never return. **Let us do good unto all, especially unto the members of the household of the faith.** To do good is the great end of life : first and most to our home, our kindred, our country, our church, our brethren in the faith, then to all men good and bad. Charity begins at home, but does not stay at home ; it goes to the ends of the earth. The church is often represented as the house of God (1 Tim. iii. 15 ; 1 Pet. iv. 17), and believers as one family, as 'fellow citizens with the saints, and members of the household of God' (Eph. ii. 19).

Autograph Warning against the Judaizers.

CHAPTER VI. 11–18.

Here the Apostle takes the pen from his clerk, and with his own hand sums up the lessons of the Epistle in a few terse, telling sentences against the teachers of circumcision (11-17), and concludes with the Benediction (ver. 18).

11 YE see how large a letter[1] I have written[2] unto you with
12   mine own hand. As many as desire to make a fair shew
    in the flesh, *a* they constrain you to be circumcised ; *b* only lest   *a* Chap. ii. 3, 14.
13 they should *c* suffer persecution for[3] the cross of Christ. For   *b* Phil. iii. 18.
    neither they themselves[4] who are circumcised keep the law ;   *c* Chap. v. 11.
    but[5] desire to have you circumcised, that they may glory in
14 your flesh. *d* But God forbid[6] that I should glory, save in the   *d* Phil. iii. 3, 7, 8.

[1] See in what large letters (characters)
[2] I write (*the epistolary aorist in Gr.*)
[3] only that they may not be persecuted on account of   [4] not even they
[5] they   [6] But as for myself let it never happen

cross of our Lord Jesus Christ, by whom [7] the world is [8] *e* cru-
15 cified unto me, and I unto the world.   For *f* in Christ Jesus [9]
neither circumcision availeth [10] any thing, nor uncircumcision,
16 but *g* a new creature.   *h* And as many as walk [11] *i* according to
this rule, peace *be* on them, and mercy, and upon *k* the Israel
of God.
17 From henceforth let no man trouble me : for *l* I bear in my
body the marks of the Lord [12] Jesus.
18 Brethren, *m* the grace of our Lord Jesus Christ *be* with your
spirit.[13] Amen.

¶ Unto the Galatians, written from Rome.[14]

e Rom. vi. 6;
chap. ii. 20.
f 1 Cor. vii.
19; chap. v.
6; Col. iii.
11.
g 2 Cor. v. 17.
h Ps. cxxv. 5.
i Phil. iii. 16.
k Rom. ii. 29;
iv. 12; ix. 6,
7, 8; chap.
iii. 7, 9, 29;
Phil. iii. 3.
l 2 Cor. i. 5;
iv. 10; xi.
23; chap. v.
11; Col i.
24.
m 2 Tim. iv.
22; Philem.
25.

[7] *or* through which (*the cross*)   [8] hath been
[9] *Many old authorities omit* in Christ Jesus (*probably inserted from v. 6*)
[10] is   [11] *The preponderating evidence is for the future* shall walk
[12] *omit* the Lord.   [13] brethren (*this word is emphatically put last*)
[14] *An error of transcribers. See Introduction.*

Ver. 11. **See in what large letters (or characters) I write unto you with mine own hand.** Not 'how large a letter' (E. V.). This would require the accusative in Greek, not the dative ('with' or 'in what large letters'). It refers to the handwriting, not to the contents. Some understand it of awkward, ill-formed characters, and trace them to Paul's inexperience in Greek (?), or to want of mechanical skill, or to defective eyesight, or to bodily suffering at the time. But the Greek (πηλίκοις) refers to large *size* only, and may indicate the emphasis laid on these concluding sentences (corresponding to our use of underscoring), or a habitual bold hand which is often expressive of energy and strong conviction. We have no autographs of the Apostles ; the oldest manuscripts date from the fourth century, and are written in large or uncial characters. Paul employed usually an amanuensis or copyist (as Tertius, who wrote the Epistle to the Romans from dictation, Rom. xvi. 22), but added with his own hand a closing benediction, or some sentences as a special mark of affection, or as a precaution against forgers of letters in his name (2 Thess. ii. 2; iii. 17, 18; 1 Cor. xvi. 21-24; Col. iv. 18; Rom. xvi. 25-27). 'I write' (lit. 'I wrote' or 'have written') is often used in epistolary style from the standpoint of the recipient. It may refer to the concluding part only, or to the whole Epistle. The former is more probable from his habit of dictating or sending a copy of his letters.

Ver. 12. **As many as desire to make a fair show in the flesh** (in the sphere of the flesh), **they** (and no others) **constrain you to be circumcised only that they may not be persecuted on account of the cross**[1] **of Christ.** They display their zeal for external or carnal ordinances by forcing circumcision upon you, that thereby they may escape the scandal and persecution of the cross of Christ, to which they would expose themselves among their unconverted Jewish countrymen by abandoning the law. (Comp. v. 11; 1 Cor. i. 24.) Circumcision and the cross, like works and faith, are antagonistic principles, if they are set up as

[1] The Greek τῷ σταυρῷ is the dative of the occasion or reason, as in Rom. xi. 20, 30; 2 Cor. ii. 13 (Gr.).

conditions of salvation. The zeal of the Judaizers is traced to a selfish motive to please men and to avoid suffering. The Pharisees loved to pray standing in the synagogues and in the corners of the streets, that they might be seen of men (Matt. vi. 5).

Ver. 13. **For not even they who are circumcised keep the law** (in all its details, comp. v. 3), **but they desire to have you circumcised, that they may glory in your flesh.** The advocates of circumcision are not sincere in their zeal, but want to gratify their vanity in making proselytes. (Comp. Matt. xxiii. 15.)

Ver. 14. **But as for myself, let it never happen (or, far be it) that I should glory** (in any thing) **save in the cross of our Lord Jesus Christ, through which** (the cross) **the world hath been crucified to me and I to the world.** The cross, as the material instrument of capital punishment of criminals and slaves, is the most ignominious of gibbets ; the cross as the symbol of Christ's passsion signifies the most glorious of facts and truths, namely, the atonement for the sins of the world. The cross of Christ was a stumbling-block to the Jews and foolishness to the heathen, and is so still to the unconverted man, because it is death to the flesh, the world, and the devil. It destroys all self-righteousness and boasting. It is the deepest humiliation of self, the strongest exhibition of man's guilt, which required even the sacrifice of the Son of God, and of God's love which made that sacrifice, and the strongest stimulus to gratitude for such amazing love. Hence Paul determined to know nothing but Christ and Him crucified (1 Cor. i. 23 ; ii. 2 ; Phil. iii. 7 ff.). Christ crucified for our sins and raised for our justification was his ruling passion, his one idea which changed his life and by which he converted others. In the cross of Christ is contained the whole redemption. 'Through which,' the cross, the instrument of Christ's crucifixion, and my crucifixion with Him (ii. 20). Others translate 'through whom,' namely, Christ ; but this would rather be expressed by 'in whom.' 'The world' alienated from God with all its vanities and sinful desires. So the word is often used by Paul and John. The world has lost all its charm and attraction for the Christian, and the Christian has lost all his appetite for the world ; they are dead to each other ; old things have passed away, Christ is all in all.

Ver. 15. **For [in Christ Jesus] neither circumcision is any thing, nor uncircumcision, but a new creature.** Comp. v. 6 and note, and 1 Cor. vii. 19. All external distinctions are lost in Christ, and the new creature is everything. In all these passages the first clause is the same, but the second differs, namely :—

Circumcision is nothing, and uncircumcision is nothing, but { faith which worketh by love (v. 6) ; a new creature (vi. 15) ; keeping the commandments of God (1 Cor. vii. 19).

'A new creature.' The Greek may mean the act of creation, or the thing created. Here the latter, as the result of a creating act of God. 2 Cor. v. 17 : 'If any man is in Christ, he is a new creature ; the old things have passed away ; behold, they are become new.' (Comp. also Eph. ii. 10, 15 ; iv. 24.) The phrase 'new creature' was common among Jewish writers to designate a moral change or conversion to Judaism (= proselyte) ; but in Paul it has a far deeper spiritual meaning.

The remarks of Luther on this verse are worth quoting as a characteristic specimen of his famous Commentary, which is not so much an exposition as an expansion and application of Paul's Epistle to the controversies of the sixteenth century. 'This is,' he says, 'a wonderful kind of speech which Paul here uses, when he says, "Neither circumcision or uncircumcision availeth any thing." It may seem that he should rather have said, "Either circumcision or uncircumcision availeth somewhat ;" seeing these are two contrary things. But now he denies that either the one or the other is of any consequence. As if he should have said, Ye must mount up higher ; for circumcision and uncircumcision are things of no such importance, that they are able to obtain righteousness before God. True it is, that they are contrary the one to the other ; but this is nothing as touching Christian righteousness, which is not earthly, but heavenly, and therefore it consists not in corporal things. Therefore, whether thou be circumcised or uncircumcised, it is all one thing ; for in Christ Jesus neither the one nor the other availeth any thing at all. The Jews were greatly offended when they heard that circumcision availed nothing. They easily granted that uncircumcision availed nothing ; but they could not abide to hear that so much should be said of circumcision, for they fought even unto blood for the defence of the law and circumcision. The Papists also at this day do vehemently contend for the maintenance of their traditions as touching the eating of flesh, single life, holy days, and such other ; and they excommunicate and curse us, who teach that in Christ Jesus these things do nothing avail. But Paul says

that we must have another thing which is much more excellent and precious, whereby we may obtain righteousness before God. In Christ Jesus, says he, neither circumcision, nor uncircumcision, neither single life nor marriage, neither meat nor fasting, do any whit avail. Meat makes us not acceptable before God. We are neither the better by abstaining, nor the worse by eating. All these things, yea the whole world, with all the laws and righteousness thereof, avail nothing to justification.'

Ver. 16. **And as many as shall walk according to this rule,** etc. Rising above all earthly distinctions to the height of Christian contemplation, Paul pronounces a benediction to all who walk according to the rule indicated in ver. 15. The Greek term for 'rule' (*canon*) is the same which is now used for the Sacred Scriptures as the rule of the Christian faith and practice. — **Peace be on them and mercy.** 'Peace' with God and with themselves, the precious fruit of the atonement and the greatest Christian blessing, which the world cannot give nor take away (John xiv. 27). 'Mercy' is coupled with peace (1 Tim. i. 2 ; 2 Tim. i. 2 ; 2 John 3). In the other Pauline Epistles we have 'grace and peace' in the salutation. — **And** (namely) **upon the Israel of God,** the true children of Israel, the people of God, as distinct from the mere carnal descendants. The believing Christians generally (not the Jewish Christians exclusively) are meant (comp. iii. 29 ; iv. 26 ; Rom. ix. 6-8).

Ver. 17. **From henceforth let no man trouble me.** Directed against the Judaizing troublers. — **For I bear in my body the marks of Jesus.** 'Marks' (stigmata) were usually letters burnt upon the arm or forehead of slaves, soldiers, criminals, also devotees of a divinity, to indicate the master, the captain, the crime, the divinity. (Comp. Rev. vii. 3 ; xiii. 16). Paul means the wounds and scars of persecution and suffering which he endured in the service of his Master, and which proved him to be a faithful bondman of Christ. (Comp. 2 Cor. xi. 23-25.) They were his credentials and his trophies. 'Of Jesus,' as the owner, the master (the genitive of possession). Much Romish superstition has been built upon the term 'stigmata,' as signifying the prints of Christ's wounds, as in the case of St. Francis of Assisi.

Ver. 18. The last sentence of this polemic Epistle is a benediction, and the last word is a word of affection, **brethren.** It takes the sting out of the severity. With all your faults, the Apostle means to say, I love you still, and the very rebuke was dictated by my deep concern for your welfare.

Thus concludes this Epistle so full of polemic fire and zeal, yet more full of grace, — free, sovereign grace, justifying, sanctifying grace, and full of forgiving love even to ungrateful pupils ; an Epistle for the time, and an Epistle for all times.

www.ingramcontent.com/pod-product-compliance
Lightning Source LLC
Chambersburg PA
CBHW022150090426
42742CB00010B/1457